TheShmuz
on Bitachon

The shmuz on Bitachon

FINDING AND KEEPING YOUR SOUL MATE

Rabbi Ben Tzion Shafier

משכן
יחזקאל
Mishkan
Yecheskel

TYPESETTING & DESIGN BY

sonnshine
publishing

ISBN: 978-1-59826-014-4

Distributed by: Feldheim Publishers
             Nanuet, NY

Printed in The United States of America

Typesetting & Design by:
             Sonnshine Publishing
             732-573-4168
             www.sonnshinedesign.com

Cover Design by Michael Silverstein

Editing by: Kressel Housman 845-371-0176

Haskamos

Divrei Bracha from
Harav Chaim Pinchos Scheinberg zt"l
on a previous Shmuz book

Rabbi CHAIM P. SCHEINBERG
Rosh Hayeshiva "TORAH ORE"
and Morah Hora'ah of Kiryat Mattersdorf

הרב חיים פינחס שיינברג
ראש ישיבת "תורה אור"
ומורה הוראה דקרית מטרסדורף

רחוב פנים מאירות 2, ירושלים, ת.ה. 6979 טל. 537-1513 (02) ישראל
2 Panim Meirot St., Jerusalem, P.O.B. 6979, Tel. (02) 537-1513, Israel

Divrei Bracha from Harav Shmuel Kamenetzky

בס"ד

שמואל קמנצקי
Rabbi S. Kamenetsky

2018 Upland Way
Philadelphia, PA 19131

Home: 215-473-2798
Study: 215-473-1212

May 3, 2012

Rabbi Ben Tzion Shafier
10 Mariner Way
Monsey, NY 10952

Dear Rabbi Shafier, שליט"א

   Thank you for sending your manuscript, the "Shmuz on Bitachon: Finding and Keeping your Soul Mate." It is written in a clear style with advice that is easy to understand. The message of bitachon is a most important one, which can greatly benefit both those searching for their zivvug and those who are already married.

   My sincere ברכה to you is that your forthcoming book will fulfill your wish to help אחינו בני ישראל find true happiness and fulfillment in their lives.

   May you be blessed with הצלחה in all your endeavors.

   J. Kamenetsky

Divrei Bracha from Harav Menachem Davidowitz

Talmudical Institute of Upstate New York

Rabbi Menachem Davidowitz, Dean
Rabbi Daniel Goldstein, Principal

OFFICERS
Rabbi Menachem Davidowitz
  President
Rabbi Shlomo Noble
  Executive VP
Michael Roth
  Treasurer
Gerald L. Segelman
  Secretary

FOUNDERS
Arnold Becker
Jack Binik
Nathan Carr
Morris Davidowitz
Morris Diamond
Abraham Feldman
Milton Fisher
S. Glick
Irving Gordon
Louis Gross
Samuel Harris
Aaron Heimowitz
Hyman Kolko
Benjamin Krieger
Barnet Levy
Leo Lisker
Hyman Mandell
Frederick Margareten
J. Bernard Merzel
Sol Merzel
William Merzel
Jerome Miller
Seymour Morris
Sydney Morris
Jack Newhouse
Goodwin Nusbaum
Harris Nusbaum
Howard I. Nusbaum
Benjamin Robfogel
Maurice M. Rothman
Irwin S. Schulman
Donald Schwartz
Soloman Schwartz
Ernest Tamary
Zev Wolfson

DIVISIONS
HIGH SCHOOL
  מתיבתא זכרון שמש
  Maurice M. Rothman
BAIS MEDRASH - KOLLEL
ADULT EDUCATION
  Anshei Kipel Volin
K-8 SCHOOL
  Derech HaTorah

March 29, 2012

The Shmuz on Bitachon: Finding and Keeping Your Soul Mate
is another powerful and dramatic presentation of the
foundations of our faith.

It is written for the 21st century reader with all of the wisdom
and color of the Shmuz on the Parsha.

May the Rebono Shel Olam help Rabbi Shafier to be able to
continue to spread the D'var Hashem.

With Torah Greetings,

Menachem Davidowitz

Rabbi Menachem Davidowitz

In Honor of Our Daughter

שרה חנה שמחה

becoming a Bas Mitzvah.
We are so proud of your middos tovos
and your accomplishments.
May the learning of this sefer serve as
a merit to enable you and all its readers
to be mekadesh shem shamayim.

Jay and Joelle Rodin

FUNDING RESOURCES

MORGAGE CORP.

LICENSED MORTGAGE BANKERS

We are proud to sponsor Rabbi Shafier's book

Shmuz on Bitachon:
Finding and Keeping
Your Soul Mate

Elly Krieger
President
NMLS #65350

In Loving Memory of our dear Husband,
Father and Grandfather,

ר׳ שרגא פייבל אריה ליב
בן ר׳ אהרן הכהן ז׳ל מאסט

Phillip Most 1932-2010

Born and raised in the Bronx during the 1930's,
שרגא פייבל was an example of one who held
true to the principals of our faith under the
guidance of his parents whom he revered with
awe. Throughout his life, his dedication and
selfless devotion to them was unparalleled, a
legacy he transmitted to his own children.

Long before America looked as it does today,
שרגא פייבל was but a rare example of an
individual who subjugated himself to those
with Rabbinical authority and maintained a
connection with רבנים throughout his life.
His resolute approach to davening with a מנין
and the עבודה he put into his actual תפילות
were a true inspiration. He lived a humble
life – never seeking recognition or credit for
his actions. He sustained these deep seated
values throughout his life even when faced
with challenges.

Table of Contents

▶ **Section One**

Marriage Is Forever 14 / The Dating Game 16 / Matchmaker, Matchmaker, Make Me a Match 19 / Men Are from Mars 24 / Infatuation Isn't a Sign That She's Bashert 28 / Love Doesn't Conquer All 30 / Hashem Wants Us to Succeed 34

▶ **Section Two**

The Difference Between Emunah and Bitachon 37 / The Miracle Called Nature 45 / Three Questions to Ask Your Local Atheist 50 / The Moment before Creation 54 / Hashem Is Involved in the Big Picture Issues of Life 60 / The Third Level of Emunah: Hashem Knows My Thoughts 68 / The Fourth Level of Emunah: Hashem Is Here 72 / Making

Your Beliefs Real 75 / Emunah and Good Luck Charms 80 / I Have Faith in You 82 / Gravity and Emunah 84 / You Can't Harm Me; You Can't Help Me 86 / Outcomes and Intentions 92 / Understanding the Decree 96 / Hashem Loves You 98 / What Did You Do to Be Worthy of Being Created? 100 / What Can You Do to Make Hashem Angry? 102 / How Much Patience Does Hashem Have? 105 / Hashem Loves You More than You Love Yourself 107 / How Smart Is Hashem? 114 / Stop Playing God 125 / What Real Bitachon Feels Like 131

▶ Section Three

The Bashert Test 134 / The Paper Test 137 / The Bashert Test 140 / Beating the System 142 / I Can't Commit 147 / Bashert Doesn't Mean That It Has to Be 150 / I Can't Find My Bashert 153 / So You Want Me to Settle? 155 / But I'm Not Madly, Passionately in Love 157 / Maybe I Missed My Bashert 160 / Keeping Your Bashert 164 / I Made the Biggest Mistake of My Life 167 / It's About Growth 169 / One Side of the Story 172 / I Never Promised You a Rose Garden 175 / The Journey's End 179

Before We Begin...

While this is a book about marriage, it is really about a much bigger issue: our relationship with Hashem.

As Jews, we are servants of Hashem. We are also called "sons" of Hashem. And, as audacious as it sounds, we are expected to have a bona fide relationship with the Creator of the heavens and the earth.

This presents a challenge. By definition, a relationship is two-sided—there's our part, and there's Hashem's part. Our part is clear; the Torah defines it in exact, specific detail. The question is: what is Hashem's part? How involved is Hashem in our lives? How much does He control?

Some things are unmistakably in Hashem's hands. No human being puts his head on the pillow at night and says, "I WILL IT TO BE THAT I WILL WAKE UP TOMORROW MORNING!" We assume that we will wake up. We hope that we will.

But we don't know, and we certainly don't control it. We accept that the big picture issues—life and death, war and disease, prosperity and the state of the economy—are in Hashem's domain.

It's the day-to-day details that aren't as clear. For instance, we're obligated to use this world in the ways of world. When we need money, we get a job. When we're sick, we go to the doctor, and not just any doctor—the best doctor that we can find. Yet we are obligated to trust in Hashem. But what does that mean? Is it our effort or is it Hashem? What if we put in too little effort? What if we put in too much? What is the balance between trusting Hashem and doing our part?

There are many questions. If Hashem decrees how many years we live, then what happens with eating right and exercising? If Hashem determines how much money we make, where does working hard fit in? If forty days before we were born a heavenly voice proclaimed the "perfect match" for each of us to marry, does that mean it has to be? Does it mean we can do nothing wrong and it will just occur? Can we pass up our *bashert*?

These are questions that a thinking person must deal with. The first step is recognizing that there is an answer. Hashem didn't just create a world, put us into it, and say, "You're on your own now. Go figure out this thing called life, and I'll see you again in 120 years."

If Hashem decrees how many years we live, then what happens with eating right and exercising?

The Torah is the blueprint for Creation. It contains all the wisdom in the world and is the manual for life—for all of life. It shows us how to conduct ourselves in the synagogue and in the street, in our business life and in our personal life. It is also a guide for understanding our relationship with our Creator, answering the most basic of questions: What does Hashem expect from us? How does He interact with us?

From that perspective, a book about how to "find your soul mate" is really about the bigger issue: how the Torah expects us to act in *this* situation. For that reason, the book you are about to read is divided into sections. The first part deals directly with the issue of marriage, outlining some of the challenges of finding and keeping a spouse. Then it takes a step back and lays out some of the most basic issues that we as Jews believe. After a thorough tour of the fundamentals, it applies those concepts directly to the issue of marriage: what to look for, what not to look for, how to maintain a marriage, and what attitudes are essential for a successful, life-long marriage.

When going through the middle section, you might catch yourself thinking, "This is an interesting work on *emunah*, but what does it have to do with marriage?" I ask for your patience. When you get to the end, I believe it will be eminently clear.

This corridor that we call life has many stages. Each is different, and each has its highlights and its challenges. Yet some are more enjoyable than others. Finding your soul mate and starting a new home is one of the most beautiful and gratifying stages of life. Often, though, it comes with a lot of anxiety and stress. How do I choose? What should I be looking for? Which issues are deal breakers and which aren't? Can I ever be certain?

Knowing that there is a right one for you, knowing that Hashem wants you to find that person, and then knowing what you should be doing to find that person, is the purpose of this book.

► Chapter One

Marriage Is Forever

I want to present you with a challenge. You have six months to find the perfect roommate. Here's how it works. You can choose anyone you want, but once you decide on this person, that's it. You're stuck—no changes. And here are the conditions. From now on, you and your roommate will do everything to-gether. You will go to sleep and get up at the same time. You will drive the same car. You will eat your meals together. You will vacation and visit family together. You will have the same friends. You will share your possessions, keep your money in the same bank account, and pay your expenses together. So what you buy, when you buy it, and how much of it you buy, you decide together. And one more thing: there will be no secrets from your

▼

roommate. You will report everything: where you go, who you go with, and how long you'll be there. This arrangement will last for four years. No taking off a semester, no two-week breaks.

How confident are you that you will make the right choice? How sure are you that you won't regret your choice after a few months?

Now, let's add one more wrinkle to this challenge. What if, instead of the arrangement lasting four years, it would last ten years? What if you now had to choose the person that you would room with for the next decade? How certain are you that you would pick the right one?

Here's the point: When you get married, it's for a lot more than ten years—hopefully, it's for life. And that's the problem. When you choose a spouse, you are committing to that person for the next who knows how long. How can you possibly make an intelligent choice? Who you are now isn't who you will be twenty years from now. People change. Things happen. And what was important to you when you were younger isn't what matters when you're older. So how can you know now who the right person will be for you when you're forty or fifty? You don't have a clue to what you will be like then.

While this is one of the more glaring difficulties with choosing the "right one," we'll soon see that there are many more.

▶ Chapter Two
The Dating Game

The *shadchan* says in that singsong voice, "So, tell me, what are you looking for?"

And out comes the laundry list.

"I need someone who is extroverted, funny, and outgoing."

"I need a woman who is very *frum*, tolerant, and kind."

"I need a *bachur* who is a take-charge type, strong but not headstrong."

The lists are long, and the benchmarks are detailed and specific. This is what I *need*. This is what I would *like*. This is what I *have to* have. If he has this quality, we can be happily married. If he doesn't, then forget it. It just won't work.

It seems that before they date, most people take a sort of personal inventory. They say to themselves, "Let's see... Since I have this type of personality, I need this type of guy. Of course, I would really like qualities A, B, and C as well. But D and E? They are non-negotiable. I just can't marry a guy who doesn't have them. If he has F and G—all the better. But for me, it's D and E. If a guy doesn't have those two, forget it. I'm just not interested."

Then, based on their understanding of what they *need*, what they *want*, and what they would *like* to have, they take that shopping list and head out into the "marketplace" to find the person who comes closest.

And, unwittingly, that is how many people make their first big mistake in dating. They aren't looking for their *bashert* (predestined match); they have already formed him in their minds, and now they're looking for the one that comes the closest to that image.

▶ Mr. Potato Head

It's almost like they are playing with Mr. Potato Head. Simply open the box and out come your choices. You can dress him up with brown eyes or blue. Big ears or small. Would you like long legs or short? What about eyebrows? Bushy or sparse? How about feet? Big or little? And don't fret—if he doesn't look exactly right, simply start over until you get him just the way you like.

This is the way people look for a spouse. They make their list, form

"Let's see... Since I have this type of personality, I need this type of guy.

their image of their ideal match, and with these convictions firmly in place, they begin their search.

Yet for some strange reason, it doesn't work. They come back empty-handed, complaining, "I just can't find the 'right one.'"

The reason they can't find the right one is that they aren't looking for him! They are too busy looking for their Mr. Potato Head—the one they created and who only exists in their imagination.

▶ Finding the Right One

The problem, however, really begins with a powerful assumption. The assumption is that the average person should know what he *needs* in a spouse. Naturally, then, his responsibility is to find the person who fits that profile.

As we will see, however, this is far from simple.

Chapter Three

Matchmaker, Matchmaker, Make Me a Match

▶ A Close Circle of Friends

When my wife and I were newlyweds, we took up an informal study of marriages. At the time, my parents had a close circle of friends, eight couples who got together regularly. We studied each couple to try and discover the "secret" to a happy marriage. After a while, we compared notes and found that we had both reached the same conclusion: each couple was mismatched!

Couple one: She was too smart for him... Couple two: He was too *frum* for her... Couple three: She was too sophisticated ... And couple four: He was too loud. Had either of us been the *shadchan*, we would never have put any of them together. They just didn't match up.

Our little exercise brought home a critical point: A successful marriage isn't a match of two *similar* individuals. It is a union of a man and woman, each with their own temperaments, emotional makeup, and personalities. Each comes in with unique strengths and weaknesses, and as a couple they complete one another. His deficiencies are compensated for by her strengths; her shortcomings are filled in by his positive attributes. The whole is much greater than the sum of the parts.

But knowing exactly what your strengths and weaknesses are and how to correctly balance them is far from simple.

▶ Who Am I?

Marriage is a complex weave of human personalities, attributes, and attitudes. Before a person can know what he needs in a spouse, he has to know himself. He has to be able to answer some fundamental questions about his personality: "Who am I? What really makes me tick? What are my core tendencies, strengths, and faults? How will I react in different life situations? How do I handle stress? What about failure? What about health issues? What if I lose a child?"

Most people don't come to this level of self-awareness until they're old and grey—and even then, not everyone does. How can we expect a young person, just starting out in life, to have such a deep understanding of himself?

But the problem is more severe. Let's assume that somehow I do know myself. To find the right match, I have to know which attributes will complement my own. Do I need a person with a strong personality or a mild one? Do I need a leader or a follower? One man may need a woman who believes in him, and another may need one who will put him in his place. But which man needs which type of woman, in what balance, and to what extent is very hard to know. As an example...

▶ The Perfect Shidduch

One day, before giving *shiur*, my *rebbe*, HaRav Henoch Leibowitz, *zt"l*, laughingly remarked, *"Baruch Hashem!* We finally found a *shidduch* for that fellow. I didn't know who we would marry him off to. What a temper he has! But, *baruch Hashem*, we found the perfect match."

At that point, while none of us knew who the *rosh ha-yeshiva* was referring to, we were very curious about the "perfect *shidduch*" for a person with a fierce temper.

The *rosh ha-yeshiva, zt"l*, continued, "We found him a woman with a temper even bigger than his. Now when he opens his mouth, she screams louder, and he's as quiet as a lamb. It's the perfect *shidduch*."

While this is a cute story, everyone knows that the worst match for a man with a temper is a woman with a bigger temper. It's asking for the next Hundred Years War...unless he only talks a big game, but is docile deep down. If his spirit is really meek, then he won't explode when confronted. Actually, quite the opposite—he will simmer down. In that case, the ideal match is a strong woman.

Which man needs which type of woman, in what balance, and to what extent is very hard to know.

But who has the wisdom to make that judgment call? Who has the life experience to know whether his inner essence will comply or rebel against such force? Certainly no other relationship requires that type of insight. When it comes to choosing a friend, the criterion is simple: do we get along? If yes—great. If not, then let's move on.

A marriage, however, is multifaceted. It entails taking two people who are diverse in nature, temperament, and upbringing, and asking them to mold themselves into one unit. Choosing the right partner requires a level of genius that the average person simply doesn't have.

In fact, most people don't even understand marriage.

▶ The Dynamics of Marriage Are Complex

Ask couples that are married for twenty years or more to explain the "secret to a happy marriage." Ask them to define why some marriages work and others don't. Why do some couples flourish and others fail?

Likely, you will get a string of answers, with most honest people admitting, "I really don't know." And if you do come across some people who are offering theories, just ask them to explain why many nice, considerate couples are at each other's throats—and plenty of coarse, selfish couples manage to get along just fine.

What you will find is that the average person can't explain these lofty mysteries because the dynamics of a successful marriage are very elusive. And even highly intelligent, worldly people can't define the "mechanics" of why a marriage works—or, if it doesn't, what to do about it. So how can we expect a young person who has never been married to know what he or she *needs* in a marriage when even older married couples can't figure it out?

If the situation isn't sounding difficult enough, there's a far bigger issue at stake.

► Chapter Four

Men Are from Mars

What really makes the notion that a young woman is capable of choosing "Mr. Right" absurd is that it denies a fundamental reality.

Hashem created men and women to serve distinct roles, and therefore, He made men and women different. Not different marginally or incidentally. Different in almost every imaginable way. They are different in their natures, outlooks, and values. They are different in the ways they approach life, objects, and relationships. They are different in the ways that they behave, relate to each other, and communicate. Men and women are so different that you would almost think that they belong to different cultures or come from different planets.

And it's not that they are socialized or brought up differently; these distinctions are inborn.

▶ Mixed Gender Best Friends

Studies show that when three-year-olds are asked, "Who is your best friend?" they are as likely to name a girl as a boy, regardless of their own gender. At that age, mixed gender friendships are the norm. Kids that young play the same games, have the same interests, and are fully compatible. Yet by the time the same group of children is five years old, only 20% of the boys will name a girl as his best friend, and the same for the girls. By then, the two groups are no longer so similar. The boys are off running around, playing rough and tumble games, and if they do sit down, it's to play with "boy toys"—trucks, action figures, and guns—things that have little appeal to the girls. By the time the same group is seven, it is almost unheard of for a boy to have a best friend who is girl, or for a girl to have a best friend who is a boy. By then, the two groups have almost nothing in common.

And these differences don't go away with age—they increase dramatically. Watch children at play during recess at the local public school. The girls will be off on one side of the yard playing jump rope or hopscotch while the boys will be off to the other side playing tag or touch football. Even though the classes are mixed, it is rare to find boys and girls together in play. The two groups have moved off into their own worlds.

So let's even assume that a young woman has enough life's wisdom to truly know herself and what type of person she needs to marry. How much does she know about the opposite gender? Is she so wise that she can *translate* her needs into the emotional language of another gender? She doesn't understand the emotional operating system of that gender. For a woman to know whether a man fits the parameters of the type she *needs*, she would have to decode a complex individual operating with a different set of feelings, needs, and desires, recognize his core strengths and attributes, and then translate that information back into her own emotional operating system. How many people have the sheer intellect to do that?

▶ Listen at the Kollel Table

If you're not sure if this is true, try visiting any *kollel*. Just listen into the conversation at the breakfast table when the newly married men talk amongst themselves. It seems that every one of them comes in with a glazed look in his eyes, mouthing the words, "I just don't understand her. When she says this, she means that. And when she says that, she means this. I just can't figure her out!"

It isn't that his wife is difficult, or that he is thick. It's simply that in the first stages of a marriage, it isn't easy to read your spouse's emotional needs. And there is a real learning curve that a husband and wife must go through to understand what is really going on in the other person's world.

▶ The Odds of Success Aren't Great

So, the plot thickens. For a person to know what it is that he needs in a spouse, he first has to fundamentally know himself. For most people, that self-knowledge doesn't develop till they are much older. Next, he has to find the corresponding jigsaw puzzle piece from amongst a gender that he doesn't understand, and then compute the differences within the context of a relationship he can't yet relate to. He will then have to make sure that this person will be suitable not just now, but also in twenty years. Finally, he has to sift through the tens of thousands of potential matches and find that one needle in the haystack.

What do you think the odds of success are?

Not good at all. In fact, for a young person to go out there and expect to find the "right one" is beyond absurd. It's preposterous.

▶ Chapter Five

Infatuation Isn't a Sign That She's Bashert

Some people will tell you that the answer must be love. "If I can't use wisdom to find my *bashert*, then I guess I have to use my heart. I'll simply go out and find the person that I fall for. If I *love* her, then obviously we are meant for each other."

And, if making their "Mr. Potato Head" is the first big mistake that people make in dating, believing that "Love Is the Answer" is the second. Here's how it plays out.

▶ Infatuation Is Not a Sign That She Is Bashert

A young man gets engaged, and his friends ask him, "How did you know that she was the right one?"

"I knew it the minute I saw her," he answers. "I took one look into her eyes, and I was gone. It was like rockets on the Fourth of July."

What this young man is describing is *infatuation*. Infatuation isn't a sign that she's your *bashert*. It is a sign that you are attracted to her. You can be attracted to your *bashert*—or to any number of people. Just ask someone who has gone out for a while. It isn't uncommon that a happily married man or woman went out with other people before they were married, and they may well have had strong feelings toward those other people, feelings that were sometimes more intense than what they felt for their spouse when they went to the *chuppah*. Yet they go on to build beautiful marriages. And equally telling, many couples get married not really being that "infatuated." Yet they create strong, loving relationships.

The reason these couples succeed isn't because infatuation isn't important—it is. But it was designed to play a specific role. To understand that role, we need a deeper perspective of the human psyche.

▶ Chapter Six

Love Doesn't Conquer All

Ask a typical, single guy what he expects his marriage to be like, and he'll get this far-off look in his eye, and will say: "Oh, it will be wonderful! I will love her, she will love me, and we'll live happily ever after."

This same young man may come from a broken home. He may have lived through years of fighting, screaming, and cursing. He may now have a difficult relationship with his parents and siblings, and may have ongoing run-ins with roommates and friends. He may even be aware that he is a difficult person—but it won't matter. His marriage will be harmony and bliss. *"My wife will love me, I will love her, and we will live together in happiness and joy forever and ever."*

Unfortunately, the divorce courts are filled with such couples. But what went wrong? They started out so in love. He was great. She was perfect. What happened?

What happened was that when they got married, they weren't in love; they were infatuated. That infatuation wore off, real life set in, and they weren't ready for it.

Infatuation is like a drug. It affects your senses and changes the way you view things. Everything is wonderful. The whole world is smiling on you. Scientific studies show that falling in love affects brain chemistry in a manner similar to cocaine use; the normal balances are changed. The result is that a couple "in love" experiences a rush of adrenaline, a sense of euphoria, and the feeling that they will always be happy together. "Her bad habits will never bother me. She will always be tolerant of my being late. And we will live forever and ever in this state of bliss."

▶ Infatuation Plays an Important Role

Hashem created infatuation to allow men and women to get married and create long-standing, loving homes. But therein lies the problem. To take two individuals from different backgrounds, with diverse natures and upbringings, put them together for a short time, and then ask them to live together for the rest of their lives in peace and harmony should be impossible.

In all relationships, differences of opinions tend to escalate, feelings eventually get hurt, and after enough time, the liaison ends. Most business partnerships end with a fight. Most friendships weaken as people go their separate ways. So the institution of marriage should never work.

To allow marriages to succeed, Hashem gave mankind the

capacity to love. When a couple is in love, they operate in a climate of acceptance and understanding. They overlook each other's shortcomings and ignore each other's flaws. She is forgiving. He is tolerant. Differences don't matter. Disagreements are rare. Your way. My way. What difference does it make anyway? And the marriage thrives despite what life throws at it. The heart blood of a successful marriage is love.

But love isn't instant. Learning to give doesn't come naturally. And real dedication to another person takes a long time to develop. To allow marriages to flourish, Hashem created certain forces to jumpstart the relationship.

One of these forces is infatuation. Infatuation works like sulphur on a kitchen match. When you strike a match against the phosphorous on the match box, it will ignite into a flame. It gets very hot, very quickly. For a second or two it will flare up, just long enough to light the wood of the match. That flame, however, wasn't designed to last. It was meant to be a catalyst to start the fire—not to keep it going. If the wood catches, it succeeded in its job. If not, it shined bright for a short while, but accomplished nothing.

Infatuation works the same way. It allows the couple to begin; it starts the process. But they must then do the difficult work of creating a true bond of love. They need to become attuned to each other's needs; they have to learn to actually care about each other. And the hardest part: they have to change those things that bother their spouse. Change isn't easy. Unfortunately, many couples never make the transition.

Love isn't instant. Learning to give doesn't come naturally.

Often, their initial expectation was their downfall. They walked in thinking, "We are in love, so everything will be beautiful and easy. *Love will conquer all.*" The problem is that they weren't in love; they were infatuated. When the drug wore off, they woke up the same people they were before, and then the choice was either change or suffer. Many people never make those changes, and their marriages dissolve.

But here is the point. While infatuation is an important tool to help start a marriage, it isn't the basis for a marriage, and it certainly isn't a criterion for choosing a life's partner. It is a short-lived chemical explosion, and if you use it as the indicator that "this is my *bashert*," you might well be making a grave error.

▶ Where Do We Go from Here?

Now we come to the crux of the issue: I can't use my wisdom to determine the right one for me because it will never work. I can't use my "falling in love" as a gauge either. So how can I know? How can I possibly decide which person is right for me?

▶ Chapter Seven

Hashem Wants Us to Succeed

The answer begins with the understanding that Hashem wants us to lead happy, productive lives. Hashem wants men and women to create loving, solid homes. And so, Hashem selects the ideal person for each individual and guides us to that person.

Our role in the equation is to do our *hishtadlus* (effort). We use the system that Hashem has set in place and do our part in finding that person. The question is: what is the correct *hishtadlus* for finding that person? How does Hashem want us to go about finding the one that He has chosen?

To answer this, we need to review some fundamentals. We need to take a look at concepts that we have known (or have been expected to know) since we were young children, and we have to ask ourselves if we truly understand them.

Let's begin with an observation. There are certain catch phrases that flip off our tongues, often without our even being aware that we uttered them.

"Have *bitachon!*"
"Hashem runs the world."
"Trust in Hashem!"

They sound so nice. So religious. The question is: do we really believe them?

"It's all for the best."
"It's always good in the end. If it isn't good, then it's not the end."

What does that mean? That all I have to do is trust in Hashem, and my life will be peaches and cream, a walk in the park? Don't people suffer? What about heart attacks? Car crashes? Cancer?

"Just have *bitachon!*"
"Keep your *emunah* strong!"

So if I have *bitachon,* it will all be good? What about divorce? Bankruptcy? What about children who die? What about terrorists?

Ironically, if you ask the typical person to explain what we're supposed to believe, they can't. What does Hashem decree? What is left to man to decide? How involved is Hashem in our decisions? Where does that leave free will?

These aren't irrelevant, highfalutin questions. These are basics that all of us must deal with on a daily basis.

"Where is your emunah and *bitachon?*"

Fine, I'll have *emunah.* I'll have *bitachon.* But would you mind explaining to me what that means?

So, before we can define the proper way to find one's *bashert*, we need to step back to define some of the most basic fundamentals. We need to clearly delineate Hashem's interaction with the world and our part in the process.

While it may take us a bit of time to get these things down pat, once we do we can then apply them to the issue at hand and to life in general.

(Please note: If you're the kind of person who can't wait for the end of the mystery story to find out "whodunnit," or if you have a date tonight, you can skip to Chapter 30 and read about the *bashert* system. But please come back here afterward. For everyone else, please hang on for a bit longer while we explore some of the basics of what we believe.)

Chapter Eight

The Difference between Emunah and Bitachon

Hashem said, "It is a shame that that which is lost can no longer be found. On many occasions, the Avos could have questioned Me, but they didn't. I told Avraham that he would be given a land that was wide and broad, and when he went to bury his wife, he had to pay an exorbitant price for a plot. Yet he didn't ask. The same with Yitzchak and Yaakov. But you, Moshe, as soon as something turns, it's 'Why have you made it bad for these people? Why have you sent me?'"

[*Sanhedrin* 111a]

Moshe Rabbeinu was sent by Hashem to redeem the Jewish people. Yet when he embarked on this mission, not only didn't the situation improve, the slavery became more intense and the pain became more profound.

Out of love for his nation, Moshe turned to Hashem and said, "Why have You worsened the situation? Why have You sent me?"

The *mefarshim* explain that Moshe was saying to Hashem, "You are the Master of the Universe. Your calculations are wise and true, and I am certain that You have a good reason to increase the Jewish people's pain. But count me out. I don't want to be a part of the oppression of my people. If it has to be done, do it without me."

While Moshe said these words out of a true love of his people, on some level it demonstrated a lack of faith in Hashem, and he was taken to task for it.

▶ Moshe Was the Single Greatest Human Being Who Ever Lived

This Gemara is difficult to understand. We know that the greatest human being who ever lived was Moshe Rabbeinu. The Rambam calls him the "father" in Torah and wisdom. One of our Thirteen Principles of Faith is that Moshe was the greatest of all *Nevi'im* (Prophets), greater than those who came before him and those who came after.

Yet this Gemara seems to imply that the *Avos* were greater. It is as if Hashem were saying, "They don't make them like they used to. Avraham, Yitzchak, Yaakov, those were great people. They trusted Me. But, you, Moshe, you aren't on their level."

How do we reconcile this with the fact that Moshe was even greater than the *Avos?*

▶ The Difference between Emunah and Bitachon

The answer to this question lies in understanding the difference between *emunah* and *bitachon.*

The Rambam defines *emunah* as the **knowledge** that Hashem created and continues to run all of Creation.

In *Shemoneh Perakim*, he writes that the first of the Thirteen Principles of Faith is: *"The Creator, blessed be He, created and orchestrates all activities, and He alone did, does, and will do all actions."*

Simply put, nothing can exist and no activity can occur without Hashem. There is no such thing as happenstance. There are no random occurrences. Hashem is intricately involved in the running of the world.

Emunah is the understanding that Hashem is involved in the big picture issues. Life and death. War and famine. Disease and disaster.

Even more significantly, *emunah* is the knowledge that Hashem is involved in the minutiae of my daily life. Hashem is there with me, 24/7, 365, all day, every day, from morning to night. No human being or other power can change my destiny. Hashem decrees the fate of man, and Hashem is there on the scene to carry out that decree.

That is *emunah:* the clear understanding that Hashem runs the

▶ *Simply put, nothing can exist and no activity can occur without Hashem. There is no such thing as happenstance.*

world, from big to little, from global to local, across all platforms and situations. Hashem is there controlling every outcome.

▶ Definition of Bitachon

Bitachon, however, is quite different. *Bitachon* means **trust.** The Chovos HaLevovos defines *bitachon* as relying on Hashem, trusting Hashem. It is a sense of depending on Him to watch over and protect me.

Hashem is kind, loving, and merciful. Hashem created me in order to give to me. And Hashem wants what is for my best. While I am responsible to be proactive, I am not in charge of the outcome, and I am not the determinant of the results. That is Hashem's role. And so, while I do my part, I rely on Hashem to care for me. *I take my heavy burden and place it on Hashem.*

Emunah is a state of *understanding.* *Bitachon* is a state of *trust.* *Emunah* comes from studying this world and seeing that there is a Creator. *Bitachon* is the state of trust that comes from recognizing that the Creator is good, kindly, and wise—and that He cares deeply for His creations.

▶ A Person Can Have Emunah and Not Bitachon

Hashem decrees the fate of man, and Hashem is there on the scene to carry out that decree.

Amazingly, a person can have *emunah* and not *bitachon.* He can know that Hashem runs the world, but not necessarily trust in Him.

Pharaoh was a classic example.

The Jews were multiplying at a fantastic rate, and the Egyptians feared that they would soon be outnumbered. Pharaoh had the solution: throw the Jewish boys into the Nile as soon as they're born. The Midrash explains that this wasn't a flippant reaction—it was highly calculated. Pharaoh said to his people, "Hashem pays back measure for measure. If we burn the babies, Hashem will burn us. If we hang them, Hashem will hang us. Hashem, however, promised Noach that He would never bring another flood. If we drown the babies, Hashem will want to punish us by drowning us, but He won't be able to. So we are safe." (*Shemos Rabbah* 1:18)

Clearly, Pharaoh understood the power of Hashem. He realized that Hashem watches over the world. He also understood that Hashem acts with justice. Pharaoh had no problem with *emunah*, but he didn't trust Hashem—he rebelled against Him. He had *emunah*, but no *bitachon*.

▶ Hashem Is Out to Get Me

I had a chance to see an example of this distinction in a setting closer to home. For many years, I was a high school *rebbe*. One day, I was speaking to a young man about some things that were going on in his life when he exclaimed, *"Hashem is out to get me!"*

I didn't know what he meant, but then he explained. "Don't you see? It's all part of a plan. I was doing so well, and then this and this happened. Just when things were starting to get better, that guy came over and did such and such. And that sent me into another tailspin. Then, just when I was getting back into things, this and this happened. Don't you see? Hashem is out to get me!"

From that point on, at least once a week, he would show me how Hashem was "out to get" him.

This fellow saw Hashem in his life, but he didn't trust Him. Quite the opposite—Hashem was the problem.

The point is that a person can understand that Hashem runs the world and still not trust Him. Even though he sees the puppeteer pulling the strings, he still may not trust the one running the show.

▶ The Avos Were Greater in Bitachon

This seems to be the answer to our question. Moshe Rabbeinu was on a higher level of *emunah* than any other human being. He saw Hashem with absolute clarity. Just as we see a piece of wood in front of us—it's there and it's real—that's the way Moshe saw Hashem. Right there.

Still, absolute trust in Hashem doesn't automatically follow. Much like a character trait that requires years to perfect, total trust in Hashem only comes with long struggles and great effort, over extended periods of time.

Apparently, the *Avos* reached a higher level in this regard. They had developed an unwavering sense of the goodness and loving-kindness of Hashem, and so they trusted him completely—even when they had questions.

Hashem promised Avraham that Yitzchak would be the father of the Jewish nation. Then Hashem told Avraham to kill Yitzchak. That was a question, a question that had no answer. But Avraham didn't ask. He trusted Hashem. Avraham was comfortable with the understanding that just because I have a question doesn't mean there isn't an answer. And just because I don't know the answer doesn't mean that Hashem doesn't have an answer. So Avraham went forward to kill his only son, with joy in his heart—fully trusting Hashem.

That is a level of *bitachon* that the *Avos* alone shared. While Moshe was greater in *emunah*, they were greater in *bitachon*.

▶ Our Belief System

This distinction has great relevance because it is the first step in understanding *emunah* and *bitachon*. It's self-evident that if a person is to practice a belief, he must understand what it is that he is expected to believe. And so, before we try to apply concepts like trusting Hashem, we need a clear definition of what *emunah* and *bitachon* are... and what they are not.

In the next number of chapters, we will try to further define these concepts according to the approach of the Chovos HaLevovos. As we explore them, we will find that there are some common mistakes—ideas and practices that many people assume are Jewish beliefs, which in fact have no connection to the Torah approach.

There is, however, a real difference between seeing a target and hitting it, so after we clearly understand the concepts, then the real work begins. For that, we need a set of exercises and growth techniques for *emunah* and a separate one for *bitachon*. Hopefully, we will map out a path for both.

It's self-evident that if a person is to practice a belief, he must understand what it is that he is expected to believe.

Let us begin by exploring the different levels in *emunah*, which really make up the basis for *bitachon*.

Chapter Nine
The Miracle Called Nature

▶ Some Serious Fundraising

Imagine that I am running a Torah organization and funds are tight. Things are so bad that it looks like we might have to close down. I decide to take action, and I'm not wasting time. I'm going straight to the top. I'm going to find myself the most famous, hidden Kabbalist in all of Israel and get a *berachah*. So I get on a plane. As soon as we land, I take a cab straight to *Tzefas*, and I find him—a direct descendant of Baba Sali. He's the real McCoy.

I enter the dimly lit, book-lined room where the Kabbalist is sitting. I approach and tell him why I came.

He looks right through me as he says, "I know about you. You are doing good work. I will help, but you must listen to what I say—exactly."

"Ah... yes, sir, absolutely," I respond.

"Take a plane back to America immediately. As soon as you land, go to Wal-Mart and buy sixty matchbox cars."

"Sixty cars?" I repeat.

"YOU MUST LISTEN!" he screams in a whisper.

"Yes, sir," I meekly answer.

"Then, take each of those cars and lay them out in the parking lot. There must be six feet between each car. When you are finished, go into a *beis midrash* and read from this parchment."

"Well... I... I uh..."

"LISTEN!"

"Yes, sir."

"And..." he adds as I open the door to leave, "when you have done as I have told you, wait one hour and open this letter. You will then understand."

I take the letter and walk out. I'm not quite sure what to make of what he told me, but, hey, I have nothing to lose. So I get back on the plane, and as soon as I land, I head straight to Wal-Mart and buy those sixty toy cars. I lay them out in the parking lot, six feet between each one. I head to a nearby *beis midrash*, say the words on the parchment, and wait.

A few minutes later, I look out the window and... "Huh?!" The cars start growing. They're getting bigger and bigger. Before long the entire parking lot is filled with cars: Cadillacs, BMWs, Jaguars...

I grab the Kabbalist's letter to see what this all means, and I read: "Now, go sell those cars and use the money well. Chazak U'Baruch."

▶ The Miracle of Nature

What if this actually happened? What if I watched a two-inch toy car grow into a full-sized SUV? What would my reaction be? I would probably fall on my face and say, "Miracle of miracles! This is astounding! It's beyond amazing!"

Yet isn't this precisely what we experience every time we put a seed into the ground? From a tiny seed comes a full-sized wheat stalk. From another grows a rose bush. From an acorn grows a fifty-foot tall oak tree. Is it any less astounding? Is it any less miraculous than a toy car growing into a vehicle you can drive?

Think about it. Fully edible food—exactly what we need for our sustenance—grows out of the ground. Corn, potatoes, cucumbers, tomatoes, beets, red peppers...

They aren't produced in factories. No one sits there figuring out the recipe or how long to leave them in the oven. All the farmer needs to do is plant the seed in the ground, and out it comes, prepared and packaged, ready to eat.

What about fruit trees? Fully developed, perfectly ripe fruit forms on its own: apples, pears, oranges, grapes, cherries...

If you ever happen to walk into a cornfield at the end of the summer and the stalks are higher than your

> *What if I watched a two-inch toy car grow into a full-sized SUV? What would my reaction be?*

head, each one laden with ears of succulent corn, ask yourself, "Where did this come from?" A farmer planted a seed, and out came a fully formed cornstalk with a husk protecting it, the sugars formed to ripen on time, and the meat of the corn split into bite-sized kernels. Isn't that a miracle?

▶ The World Screams Out to Its Creator

When you study nature, you see the Creator. When you look at the world around you and contemplate its many harmonious systems, all integrated, all perfectly in balance, you see Hashem.

For example...

Imagine you are seated in an ornate concert hall. The upholstery is stately, the ambiance thick. Suddenly, the house lights dim. The stage is dark. Slowly, the curtains lift, and a train of smartly dressed musicians take their places behind the eighty-one instruments arranged on the stage.

On cue, the symphony begins. First the wind instruments, then the brass; slowly the strings join in, and then the percussion. The music is heavenly. The unity of it all, the perfect symmetry is breathtaking. Your reverie is interrupted by the fellow sitting next to you as he says, "It's amazing that they play so well without a conductor."

"What do you mean?" you respond.

"I mean, no conductor. There's no one leading them. They're just playing."

"What makes you say that?"

"Simple. I looked on stage. I don't see a conductor. So obviously, there is none."

Just because this fellow's view is blocked doesn't mean the conductor isn't there. Someone wrote the music. Someone hired the musicians. They didn't just all show up one day, randomly start playing, and there it was—Mozart's fifth concerto! The harmony, the precision, the synchrony, all demonstrate the conductor's existence.

Yet, astonishingly, people stare at the wonders of Creation and mouth the words, "I guess it just happened." A lucky roll of the cosmic dice.

And sometimes you just have to wonder: are these people serious when they say things like this? Do they really mean it? You might even be tempted to ask them straight out, "Do you really believe that it all just happened by itself?"

Nothing in human experience just happens. Buildings don't just materialize; they require teams of architects, planners, and builders to erect them. Corporations don't just evolve; they demand coordinated teams of employees, salespeople, accounting personnel, and managers to maintain them. Computer programs don't create themselves; cadres of hundreds, sometimes thousands of people meet, discuss, plan, and then execute the coding.

Yet you expect me to believe that something so many times more sophisticated than anything that man has ever designed just randomly occurred? No wisdom, no forethought, no one guiding it? On its own, it just evolved! Kind of makes you wonder...

So, the next time you get into a conversation with your local atheist, here are three questions you can ask him.

Chapter Ten

Three Questions to Ask Your Local Atheist

Imagine you are standing in an orchard filled with orange trees in full blossom. The branches are heavy with ripe, succulent oranges stretching out as far as the eye can see. The farmer explains that a mere ten years ago, it was a barren field. Over time, he planted the rows and rows of seeds, which grew into all those orange trees.

Let's think about this for a moment. Each mature orange tree began as a small white seed planted in the ground. That seed weighed a mere fraction of an ounce. But an orange tree weighs thousands of pounds.

Here is question number one to ask your local atheist: *Where did the thousands of pounds of stuff that make up the tree come from?* The roots, the trunk, the branches—thousands of pounds of matter. Where did it all come from?

If you are tempted to say that it must have come from the ground, I'm afraid you'd be wrong. If you were to take a large steel vat, fill it with five hundred pounds of soil, plant an orange seed in that soil, and come back ten years later, you would find a fully-formed orange tree weighing thousands of pounds and the same five hundred pounds of soil remaining in the vat. The stuff that makes up the tree doesn't come from the ground at all.

It is created through photosynthesis. The leaves absorb the sunlight, mix in some carbon dioxide and water, and synthesize the various materials. Synthesis, of course, is the operating word. It's the process by which existing elements are manufactured into something new, something not there before. The chlorophyll in the leaves forms the chemicals and compounds and puts them together in perfect order. From thin air, it creates the bark, the wood, and the specialized plant cells needed to transfer water from the roots to the leaves.

Interesting. If you owned a factory that could create stuff out of nothing, you'd be doing pretty well.

But it gets more interesting when we look at the orange itself.

When you bite into an orange, you get that sort of sweet, sort of tangy, citrusy taste. Here is question number two to ask your local atheist: *Where did the taste of the orange come from?*

Everything about the orange began from that little seed. But when you bite into that pit, it's bitter.

If you owned a factory that could create stuff out of nothing, you'd be doing pretty well.

The water that feeds the tree is tasteless. The ground that the tree grows in is also tasteless. So if the pit is bitter, and the water and ground are tasteless, where does the sweetness in the orange come from?

The answer, again, is photosynthesis. The chlorophyll in the leaves act as photoreceptors that capture the energy in the sunlight to create carbohydrates. These carbohydrates are then synthesized (there's that word again, creating something new) into the sugars, the tang, and flavors needed to form the sweet citrus mix. Pretty impressive stuff for a leaf, no? Have you ever given an IQ test to a leaf? "Uh, excuse me, can you tell me the PH level of orange juice, and who is currently the President of the United States?"

(Please note: there are no little elves inside the tree telling it how to mix the formula. "A bit more sugar, not so much tang. Hey, go easy on the pulp there.")

But things get even more bewildering when we look at the orange itself. You see, the orange is a distinct color—orange. And this brings us to question number three. The pit is white. The water is colorless. The ground is brown. *Where did the orange color come from?*

If you dig down as far as China, you won't find orange coloring in the ground. So where did it come from?

You guessed it: photosynthesis. The leaves process some of the sucrose they create into the coloring needed for the skin. Not red—that's the color of apples. Not green—that's for pears. Not purple—that's for plums. Orange.

Now, quick: which colors combine to make orange? What percentage red? How much yellow? What is the chemical composition of pigment?

(Please note: only the outside skin of an orange is colored. That part is visible and creates the eye appeal, so color there serves a purpose. But the inside of the skin doesn't make the fruit more attractive; it would be useless to color it. And so, it is white.)

Now, don't get all excited here. Don't go invoking words like astonishing, amazing, stupendous... Just remember: it's nature, plain and simple. There was a lucky role of the cosmic dice, and a hundred billion galaxies, each containing a hundred billion stars, came into being—just like that.

And each of those stars churns out unfathomable amounts of energy. Our own sun (a smallish star) transmits so much energy that despite its being over ninety million miles away, it heats our planet and warms our oceans. And even though only two billionth of a percent of its energy ever reaches here, it fuels all of life and growth on earth. And, of course, it does all this through that lucky process called photosynthesis.

And for this to function, there has to be a whole host of other processes in place: the laws of organic chemistry and biophysics, the rules governing light properties and its conversion into energy. Hosts and hosts of complex interwoven systems are all being executed flawlessly time after time, in all locations throughout the cosmos.

What a thinking person sees is that nature is the greatest indicator of the Creator. It is the firmest proof to His existence.

You might be wondering why we need to focus on this. We believe; we accept that Hashem created the world and all that it contains. So what does all this have to do with us?

> Chapter Eleven
The Moment before Creation

It has a lot to do with us when we think about the moment before Creation, when all of this wasn't. The universe wasn't. Space wasn't. Earth wasn't. Matter and energy weren't. Hashem said, "It should be," and it became.

Energy sprang forth. Matter happened. Time itself began. Then light and darkness. Next the moon, the sun, and the stars.

▶ What Color Was It?

When my daughter was six years old and we were discussing Creation, there was one issue that she couldn't come to terms with. "Abba," she said, "I understand that before Hashem created the world there was nothing, not even light and dark, but what color was it?"

The difficulty she was having is that we are so used to the world as it is that the concept of *before Creation* is hard to imagine. The idea of the absence of anything—before there was a world, before there was even matter, space, or any substance to hold it in—is difficult for us corporeal beings to fathom. We keep falling back to our way of viewing things in a physical setting, and absolute void has no place in our world.

But let's try for a moment to envision a vast empty nothingness. There is no space, no matter. There isn't even time because time only exists in a physical world. And Creation begins. Out of nothing—because there is nothing. From nowhere—because there is no place. At this absolute first moment in time, Hashem brings forth matter, the very building blocks of Creation. Then come darkness and light, not even separated, but intermingled—a patch of light here, a flash of darkness there. Next come the heavens and the earth, then the planets and the stars, the fish in the sea, the birds in the sky, and all of the animals of the earth. And on the final day, at almost the last moment of Creation, comes man.

▶ Ex Nihilo Creation

This is unlike anything in our experience... and it's a point that is often missed. When man builds a house, he claims to have made something new. Yet in reality, he *created* nothing. The wood was already in existence. The rocks were already there. Along came man with a shovel and ax, moved things around, and claimed he *created* something new. Yet all he did was rearrange things already created.

An analogy to this would be:

▶ Frank the Cookie Baker

Every day, when Frank leaves work, he brings home two packages of freshly baked cookies for his kids. His children love to brag about the delicious cookies their father makes. Frank's kids are the envy of the entire first grade. Naturally, when the class is planning a bake sale, who do they ask for help with the recipes? Frank!

Unfortunately, Frank doesn't know that much about recipes or baking cookies. You see, Frank works in a factory. Every morning, at exactly 4:20 AM, Frank turns the switch that starts the machine, and exactly thirty-five minutes later, out roll the first batch of *Stella D'oro Chocolate Fudge Cookies.*

Frank didn't create the process; he doesn't even know which ingredients go into the dough. He wouldn't be able to tell you the different preservatives and flavorings that are used. He can't explain the difference between radiant and convection heat and their effect on the crispness of the cookie. He certainly isn't capable of creating the intricate system of conveyer belts, mixers, and feeder chain ovens needed to produce that cookie. His job is to flip the switch. The machine does the rest.

▶ Creative in Name, But Not in Principle

When a couple has a child, they use a system that Hashem put into place to bring forth a baby. They don't claim to be knowledgeable enough in anatomy to synthesize the proteins needed for growth. They don't allege to have sufficient understanding in physiology to weave the neuron pathways in the brain. And they certainly don't contend that they are learned enough in pathology to create the immune system that develops within their fetus.

When we use the term *made a baby*, we mean the parents used a pre-existing system that was set up with great wisdom and forethought. They pushed the button, and the gears and flywheels went into motion. Nine months later, a perfectly-formed, complex marvel called a human was born. They *had* the baby, but they didn't *create* the baby.

This is true of any creative act that a human engages in, whether it be a couple having a child, a farmer growing corn, or an entrepreneur creating an industry. We take pre-existing elements, use pre-formed systems, turn a switch... and then take the credit for the result. In our minds' eye, it is our effort that brought forth the product, but in reality, we did little but use the machinery already in place.

Hashem alone is the Creator. From nothing, He brought forth everything. And He alone conceived of, designed, and formed all of it. Every element had to be thought out; there were no givens. There was no imitating or accepting the status quo, because before Creation, there was nothing to imitate or use as a model.

When we take this huge leap of understanding, we begin to recognize the wonders that are all around us and the wisdom that is manifest throughout Creation. Most importantly, from this we gain a glimpse of Hashem. The house itself attests to its Creator.

> *We take pre-existing elements, use pre-formed systems, turn a switch... and then take the credit for the result.*

From this perspective, nature, science, and the world itself are sources of constant inspiration. The more I understand the wisdom of the world, the more I perceive the greatness of its Creator. By focusing on this, I see Hashem with greater clarity day by day.

▶ Why Aren't We Moved by This?

In actuality, we should be so moved by nature that we should have a constant stream of inspiration. We should want to sing out praise to its Creator all the time. And yet, it doesn't move us. We live with it, and it doesn't affect us.

One of the reasons is that we are so used to it. Of course, the sun rises; it has done so every day of my life. Of course, the oceans never exceed the shore; it's been that way ever since I can remember. Of course, the chicken comes out of the egg. Doesn't it always?

And so, nature, as astounding as it is, loses its impact. It loses its wow.

▶ WOW — Wonders of the World

To help put some of the wow back into nature, we need to look at nature and its wonders with new eyes. We need to approach it as if it didn't have to be that way. If we view it from the right perspective, we will comprehend the wisdom that went into creating the world; we will appreciate the care with which everything came into being. More than anything, we will see our Creator. Not in some maybe, kind of, quasi way. We will see Hashem—right there.

And this is the first level of *emunah:* knowing that the world has a Creator, knowing that originally there was nothing. Then Hashem said it should be, all of physicality sprang into being.

But this is only the first level of *emunah*; there are three more. Let's move on to the next.

Chapter Twelve

Hashem is Involved in the Big Picture Issues of Life

> *On Rosh Hashanah it is written, and on Yom Kippur it is sealed: how many will pass from the earth, and how many will be born. Who will live, and who will die. Who will die at his predestined time, and who before his time. Who by water, and who by fire...*
>
> [*Tefillas Rosh Hashanah*]

The second level of *emunah* is knowing that Hashem is involved in the big picture issues of life. Which nations will go to war and which will enjoy peace? Which totalitarian dictators will threaten world destruction? How much havoc will they be permitted to wreak? Which countries will prosper and which will suffer? Which political figures will suddenly pop up on the scene? Which names that yesterday were unknown will suddenly and menacingly take center stage? Which new technologies will be brought to the marketplace? Which diseases will suddenly appear? Which cures will be discovered?

All of the issues of the coming year are reviewed, assessed, and decided by Hashem.

If you visualize the planet as a multi-dimensional chessboard, Hashem sits as the Grand Master, mapping out the moves of the coming year. This pawn will go here; this one there. This knight belongs here; the bishop over there. All of the events of the coming year are weighed, measured, and determined.

In simple terms, the headlines of the *New York Times* are written on Rosh Hashanah. But it isn't only the headlines of the coming year that are written; every article, every feature story, and every news scoop from the global down to the local is written down as well.

The *New York Times* recently reported that it employs 350 full-time reporters and hundreds of freelance contributors in fifty-three distinct news bureaus divided into local, national, and foreign territories. A single Sunday edition of the *Times* has more words than the entire Tanach, and reading it aloud would take over twenty hours.

Why is that? Because there are many, many issues that affect the over six and a half billion people on earth. And every one of them is planned out by Hashem on Rosh Hashanah. Hurricanes and tsunamis, earthquakes

A single Sunday edition of the **Times** *has more words than the entire* **Tanach.**

and famines, terrorist attacks and ponzi schemes. While Hashem gives man free will, it is only in regards to our choices. Each and every outcome remains in Hashem's hands.

Looking at the world from this viewpoint leads to a sense of order and calm. There is a Master to the house. Anything that transpires has been weighed and measured. While I may not know all of the reasons, there is a plan and there is a purpose. I see Hashem running the events of the world, and I no longer fear super powers and economic collapse. Al Qaeda and Ahmadinejad, Hezbollah and Hamas—they are the puppets, and Hashem is pulling the strings. And so, I read the newspapers with almost joyful anticipation. I can't wait to see what Hashem has in mind.

▶ Closer to Home

From this perspective, I should feel a great sense of jubilation on Rosh Hashanah. We, the Jewish People, are servants of Hashem, and we are also His fans. We are His Chosen Nation, and He is our Master. During the course of the year, we suffer through the insolence and audacity of arrogant people who deny Hashem's rule and control over the world. On Rosh Hashanah, we revel in the fact that Hashem sits as the true Judge, meting out the fate of mankind. As such, we should feel a tremendous sense of joy, an outpouring of emotion as we contemplate the magnificence of the *Din*.

This is the day that humanity's fate is decided. My Creator sits as the Judge. He alone determines what will transpire in the coming year. I trust in His kindness and His wisdom. And so, I feel a sense of tranquility and joy. The house is in order; the Master is home.

Nevertheless, that emotion has to be tempered. While it's grand to recognize that mankind as an entity is being judged, I, too, am a man, and I, too, am being judged. My fate for the coming year is in question. Will I live or die? Will I be healthy or sick? Will I enjoy great prosperity or not? The fate of my family, the fate of my community, and the fate of my loved ones is being decided.

▶ Understanding Life Settings

Before a man is born, Hashem sets a life for him. He will live so many years, enjoy this level of well-being, and have this amount of success. That is his life setting. Each year, those issues are revisited.

Before I was put onto this planet, I may have been granted 120 years. The question is: am I now worthy of that? Based on who I am now, is that good for me? I might have been originally slated to enjoy great financial success, but am I now the type of person who will use my wealth wisely or not? The issues that are decided on Rosh Hashanah encompass the breadth of the human experience. Each person is judged, each is measured, and his fate is set.

So while I should feel jubilation on this day, it needs to be tempered by a sense of awe. My future is being decided. But both emotions should be there—great joy mixed with trepidation.

▶ It Is Hard to See the Judgement

With this as a backdrop, here is an observation.

We are told over and over about the power of prayer. We know that Hashem is more merciful than any person we could ever imagine. And Chazal tell us that Hashem waits for our prayers.

If we accept that our fate for the coming year is decided on Rosh Hashanah, then we should spend the entire day in *shul* with tears streaming down our cheeks, imploring, beseeching, begging Hashem for mercy. While it's true that the *davening* on Rosh Hashanah is more intense than usual, for most people crying and begging isn't an apt description. The question is: why?

Part of the reason is that the judgment on Rosh Hashanah is different than any other judgment that we experience. As an example:

▶ A Mockery of Justice

In 1994, O.J. Simpson was on trial for murder. The case drew great interest because, in a sense, the U.S. Judicial system was on trial. To anyone reading the news objectively, it was clear. The man killed his wife. The question was: could money, fame, and bias sway the jury? A dream team of lawyers was called in to defend him. And after months of high acrobatics, a decision had been reached.

The day that the verdict was read, O.J. Simpson sat in court gripping the bench. His entire future was being proclaimed. Would he spend the rest of his life behind bars, or would he again be free?

> **The judgment on Rosh Hashanah is different than any other judgment that we experience.**

The jury foreman rose to read the verdict. "We find the defendant... not guilty."

Simpson's face lit up. The joy, the relief, the happiness was palpable.

▶ The Verdict Is Read

That is judgment in this world. There is a period of fact-finding, a period of deliberation, and then the decision is read for all to hear. At that point, the judge, the jury, the defendant, and all in attendance know the ruling.

We live through a similar process on Rosh Hashanah. There is a period of fact-finding and a period of deliberation before the verdict is reached. But we don't hear the verdict. We don't know what the decree is.

Were we given a year of life or not? Were we granted a year of health and well-being or not? The decree is set, but we don't hear it. If we did, it would change the way we view life.

▶ What We Don't See

The Steipler Gaon, *zt"l*, was known as a man of extraordinary holiness and was accepted as one of the leaders of his generation. People would come to him from far and wide for advice or a *berachah*. Often, they would hear words that bordered on prophetic.

One day, a man walked into the Steipler's small apartment in Bnei Brak. It was midafternoon, and there were already many people on line waiting. Typically, the Steipler would sit at his desk and listen to the person who had come to see him for a moment or two, his eyes largely remaining on the *sefer* in front of him. It was rare for the Steipler to look up. When this man walked into the apartment, not only did the Steipler look up, he stared directly at him, and in Yiddish began shouting at him, "*Rasha, rasha* (wicked one), get out! Get out, *rasha!*"

Everyone in the room was silent. All eyes turned to this man. He turned red. He turned white. Then he ran out of the apartment.

A few hours later, someone came in to see the Steipler and said in a low voice, "*Rosh Yeshiva*, forgive me, but that man that the Steipler called a *rasha* doesn't seem to be such a *rasha*. When he left the Steipler's apartment, he got into a car that had a number of other people inside. The car got into a major crash, and every other person in the car died. He was the only one that was unhurt. Obviously, he isn't such a *rasha*!"

The Steipler responded, "Don't you understand? When he walked into the room, the Angel of Death walked in with him. I didn't have a choice. When someone humiliates his friend, it's as if he killed him. That was the only way I could save him."

There used to be a time when men like the Steipler could see the Angel of Death. We can't. So it is difficult for us to relate to the issues that are decided on Rosh Hashanah.

▶ Seeing the Din

Nevertheless, when you look around an average *shul* on Rosh Hashanah, you should recognize that many decrees are being put into place. There will many beautiful pronouncements. That man who lost his job and can barely pay his bills will be granted a year of great financial well-being. That older single who has not yet found her *bashert* will be granted to meet him this year. The couple that has not yet merited having children will now be granted a child.

> *"Don't you understand? When he walked into the room, the Angel of Death walked in with him."*

There will, however, also be many decrees that aren't so pleasant. That man will lose his business. This family will go through great travails. That woman will be stricken with a dreaded illness. And if you *daven* in a large enough congregation, there will also be a few people who will get an X over their heads. This will be their last year of life; they won't make it to next Rosh Hashanah.

But we don't see this. We walk out of *shul* on Rosh Hashanah, and we wish each person a good sweet year. But we don't know. We don't know what the decree is. We don't know what the outcome will be.

But we understand that Hashem knows what is best. Hashem sits as the Ultimate Judge, and Hashem metes out mankind's fate.

And this is the second level of *emunah:* knowing that Hashem determines mankind's fate. We humans seem so powerful. We aren't. We don't control the outcome. Hashem is in charge.

The first level of *emunah* is knowing that Hashem created and maintains all of physicality. The second level is knowing that Hashem is involved in the actual running of the world. The third level of *emunah*, however, is a bit more difficult for us mortals. To illustrate let's use a parable.

Chapter Thirteen

Chapter Thirteen
The Third Level of Emunah: Hashem Knows My Thoughts

Imagine that you hear about a rabbi from Monsey. Rumor has it that he's a real nice man. In fact, every Friday afternoon he helps out an old widow. He shops for her. He does her laundry. He even gets on his hands and knees to scrub her floors. You are very impressed; he sounds like a real *tzaddik*.

> **My intentions don't color my actions—they define them.**

But then you find out one little detail. It seems that this poor, old widow has no living heirs and owns an estate worth fifteen million dollars. *Oh... big tzaddik!*

Here is the point: my intentions don't color my actions—they define them. If my intentions are to help an unfortunate woman, then it is a commendable act. If my intentions are to walk off with someone's fortune, then it's deplorable. My intentions determine what the act is.

With this understanding comes a powerful recognition. If I believe in reward and punishment, then I believe that Hashem knows my thoughts. Because if Hashem doesn't know my thoughts, there can be no justice. It's not just *what* I did that matters—it's *why* I did it. What did it mean to me? Was my act pure or selfish? Self-centered or not?

If I believe that at the end of my days, I will be richly rewarded for what I did right and held accountable for what I transgressed, then I accept that Hashem knows my intentions.

▶ We Think We Know

One of the ironies of life is when we play judge and jury of others. We make all types of assumptions about other people's upbringing and background. We take it as a given that we know what's going on in their lives. And then we reach value judgments about the person and his actions. Yet how often do we find out that we really don't have a clue?

▶ A Small Shteibel

A number of years ago, the members of a small *shul* were asked not to bring little children to the Rosh Hashanah *davening*. It was a small building, and they wanted a higher level of decorum. As there were a number of other *shuls* in close proximity, they asked that anyone who wished to bring their little children to *shul* to please go to one of the other choices. The notices went out, and signs went up. Everyone knew the policy.

On Rosh Hashanah day, the *gabbai* was in *shul* with his *tallis* over his head, absorbed in prayer. Right after *Barechu*, in walked a man with five little boys in tow. Together, they made their way across the *shul* to the row right in front of the *gabbai*. The man sat down and, one by one, the five little boys plunked down, too.

The *gabbai* was furious. He'd sent out the e-mails. He'd put up the signs himself.

"How can he just walk in here," he screamed to himself, "and sit down as if nothing's wrong?!"

But it was the middle of *davening* on Rosh Hashanah. The *gabbai* didn't say anything.

After a few minutes, the candies started coming out, the wrappers getting noisily tossed around. It wasn't long before one child was nudging the one next to him. That one nudged him back. Back and forth. Back and forth. By now, the *gabbai* was livid.

"The nerve! Some people..." he thought to himself. "But still, it's Rosh Hashanah."

And he did everything he could to hold his tongue.

It wasn't until a little while later when that man and his five sons stood up to say *Kaddish* that things became clear. It turned out that a woman in the community had passed away a few days before. The man didn't see the signs because he was sitting *shivah* for his wife. His sons were sitting *shivah* for their mother. Then the *gabbai* was very glad that he held his tongue.

We think we know where other people are holding. We think we know what their challenges and tests are. We don't.

But if I accept that Hashem is the True Judge, then I accept that Hashem knows my intentions. Hashem knows my past; He knows me since before I was born. He knows my nature and my personality. He knows what I have worked on and what I still need to work on. And He knows exactly what any given situation means to me.

As an illustration, most school science labs have a transparent model of a man. You can peer right into him. There are his kidneys. There are his heart, his lungs, and his pancreas.

That is an apt parable for us. When we stand in front of Hashem, we are transparent. Hashem peers into the essence of us and knows exactly what we are thinking as we think it.

This concept shouldn't be foreign to us. We end every *Shemoneh Esrei* with the *pasuk: "May the words of my lips and the thoughts of my heart be pleasing to You."* (*Tehillim* 19:15)

With those words, I acknowledge that Hashem knows my thoughts. When I *daven*, I don't have to speak the words out for Hashem to hear them. My words are for myself. Hashem knows exactly what I want to say.

So if the first level of *emunah* is knowing there is a Creator, and the second level is knowing that Hashem is involved in the running of the world, this is the third level of *emunah:* knowing that Hashem reads right through me.

Nevertheless, while these three levels are very significant and even vital to our understanding life, they are far removed from our ordinary experiences. They won't affect us in our day-to-day activities. It is the fourth level of *emunah* that is the key to everything that we believe in, and is also the most difficult to put into practice. To understand that level, we need to look carefully at a verse in the Torah.

Chapter Fourteen

The Fourth Level of Emunah: Hashem Is Here

> "And Yaakov feared greatly, and it caused him pain, and he split the nation that was with him, the sheep, cattle, and camels into two camps."
>
> [Bereishis 32:7]

▶ Aisav Comes to Kill Yaakov

The word came to Yaakov that his brother Aisav was coming to greet him, accompanied by four hundred men—armed to the teeth. It was obvious to all that Aisav intended to kill Yaakov. The *pasuk* tells us that Yaakov feared greatly.

In *Berachos* 4a, R' Yaakov bar Idi asks how this is possible. When Yaakov was leaving his father's house, Hashem promised him that he would be protected. So how was it possible that Yaakov was now afraid?

R' Yaakov bar Idi answers that Yaakov was afraid that Hashem's promise was based on who he was back then and would only apply if he'd remained on that level. Yaakov feared that he might have sinned and was no longer the same man he used to be, and so the promise no longer applied. Therefore, he was now afraid of Aisav.

▶ Putting This into Perspective

This Gemara becomes difficult to understand when we take into account that after all is said and done, Yaakov Avinu was still a human being. No matter how great the *Avos* were, they were made out of the same flesh and blood that we are. They had the same physical makeup that we do, and they faced all the challenges of being human.

This means that Yaakov had that most difficult challenge of life: integrating his intellectual understanding into practice in life, of *believing* and *not believing*. Of course, he knew that Hashem promised to protect him, but now he faced his brother—a powerful, driven man who had a burning desire to settle an old grudge. And he wasn't coming alone; he'd brought with him an army to aid in what was his clear intention—murder. So why does R' Idi assume that it was impossible for

Hashem promised him that he would be protected. So how was it possible that Yaakov was now afraid?

Yaakov to be afraid? Maybe Yaakov was just scared, not because of any sin that changed his level, but because of the danger that he faced. Perhaps he was afraid of Aisav, afraid of being out there alone, and afraid of dying.

▶ Hashem Made That Promise Thirty-Four Years Ago

What makes this question even stronger is that Hashem's promise to Yaakov was made over thirty-four years before Aisav came to greet him. An awful lot of time had passed since Yaakov left his parents' home. Perhaps his trust in Hashem's promise had faded over time. Perhaps Yaakov was ever so slightly affected by the ways of the world. Why does R' Yaakov bar Idi assume that there must be some answer as to why Yaakov was afraid? The explanation might be quite straightforward: Yaakov hadn't heard this promise in many, many years, and he was simply afraid. Maybe Yaakov was much like us.

To answer this question, let's turn to a modern day example.

► Chapter Fifteen

Making Your Beliefs Real

Imagine you are walking down a dimly lit street. It's the middle of February, late at night, and you're in a part of town you don't normally frequent. You look around — not a soul to be seen.

"It's mighty quiet," you think to yourself. You tighten your coat and walk a bit quicker, listening to the loud click of your heels hitting the sidewalk.

Suddenly, SCREECH! A car jerks to a stop, directly in front of you. Three thugs jump out. They surround you. One of them reaches into his pocket, pulls out a gun, and points it at your head.

You've never stared down the barrel of a gun before—at least not a real one. Suddenly, you realize that your life is in the hands of this punk. Whether you live or die is in the control of this drug-crazed kid who doesn't care about you... or anything else for that matter.

Now, imagine that this little scenario has a happy ending, and somehow you make it home that evening, alive and unhurt. After the initial shock wears off, you find yourself face to face with a major philosophical problem. Since the time you've been a little kid, you've accepted that Hashem runs the world. You even remember being taught that on Rosh Hashanah, Hashem decrees who will live and who will die.

Yet what good is that decree when your life was clearly in the hands of that punk? In fact, what good is any judgment that Hashem sets when so many things "just happen?" People get sick. Drunk drivers plow into innocent pedestrians. Lone cancer cells invade healthy men.

▶ Hashem Is on the Scene

The answer to this quandary is that if you accept that Hashem decrees who will live and who will die, then you accept that Hashem is there to carry out that decree. If you recognize that Hashem determines your destiny, then you recognize that Hashem is with you on the scene, 24/7, to carry out His will.

This concept has dramatic ramifications. It means that Hashem is with you throughout your day. He's there when you get out of bed in the morning and when you close your eyes at night, when you walk down the stairs and when you get behind the wheel of your car. All day, every day, morning and night—Hashem is there, watching, guarding, and orchestrating the events of your life.

While it is true that Hashem controls the constellations, the planets, and the stars, it's far more relevant that He controls your life. Supervising, influencing, and directing all that happens. There are no *happenstances*, no random occurrences, no lucky rolls of the dice. Everything, *everything*, is directed by His will.

And implicit in this is another major recognition. If on the previous Rosh Hashanah it was decided that your time is up, then there is nothing that you or anyone else can do to change that. It's curtain time, game over. However, if the determination was that you should enjoy another year of life, there is also nothing that anyone can do to change that. Not powerful people. Not rich people. Not influential people. And not punks carrying big guns.

Either the kid will drop the gun, or it will misfire, or some cab driver will decide to turn down that street, or the entire NYC Fire Department will show up on a false alarm. There are many, many messengers that Hashem uses to do His bidding. But it is Hashem on the scene, carrying out His decree.

▶ Yaakov Walked with Hashem

This seems to be the answer to the question of why it is not possible that Yaakov's fear was just plain fear of Aisav.

One of the key distinctions between Yaakov Avinu and the average person is that Yaakov walked with Hashem. When he got up in the morning, he said, "Good morning, Hashem." When he went

There are many, many messengers that Hashem uses to do His bidding. But it is Hashem on the scene, carrying out His decree.

to sleep at night, he said, "Good night, Hashem," because his Creator was directly in front of him. When he went about his daily activities, Hashem was with him all day long. Hashem was there as he walked, as he ate, and as he greeted people.

One of the reasons that we have such difficulties in trusting in Hashem is that Hashem isn't "here." Perhaps Hashem is some thirteen billion light years away, up in the heavens. But when I am walking on a cold, dark street, late at night, I am alone. It is those three punks against me. So naturally, I am afraid. Who wouldn't be?

▶ Yaakov Avinu Was Never Alone

But Yaakov Avinu was never alone. His entire existence was focused on being close to Hashem. Hashem was present with him every moment of his day. When he went to the well to find a wife, Hashem was right there, arranging for Rachel to come along with the sheep. When he went to the house of Lavan, Hashem was right there, protecting him from the scheming of a trickster. And now that he was preparing to meet his brother in what was likely to be mortal combat, he was not going out alone. He was with Hashem. And so, Yaakov wasn't afraid.

It would be the equivalent to you and me walking down the street accompanied by the entire US Marine Corps when some high school punk pulls out a switchblade and threatens us. Would it be possible that we would be afraid? This was R' Idi's question. Since Yaakov saw Hashem with him all day, every day, right there, how could he fear a mortal man? The only possible answer is that he was afraid that Hashem's promise was no longer in effect.

▶ The Ramifications of This Are Profound

This is the fourth level of *emunah:* knowing that Hashem is here. Hashem is with me throughout my day—when I learn, when I *daven*, when I eat, when I sleep. Hashem occupies every part of the universe. Wherever there is physicality, there is Hashem.

This concept is life-changing. It affects every aspect of our existence in ways far larger than we might realize. It brings us to a different understanding of life and our relationship with Hashem. It allows us to view situations, people, and events in a vastly different manner.

And it is the basis of our entire belief system. Because, without this, nothing we believe in makes any sense.

▶ Chapter Sixteen

Emunah and Good Luck Charms

A generation ago, bingo games were serious fundraisers for Torah institutions. Most *yeshivas* ran them, and as the staff at the game could only be volunteers, many a *yeshiva bachur* found himself "volunteering" to work the game.

Every game had its version of Sadie: an older woman in a housecoat, sitting at the end of the third row. On the table were her good luck charms—her lucky rabbit foot keychain, her lucky pennies, her winning card from last month—all laid out in exact "lucky" order. And she sat there waiting for her special number to be called.

"I-19."

"I-19. That's my number!" she'd cry as she held her rabbit foot even closer for better luck.

There are many people who might tell you to have *bitachon*, but what they really mean is something like Sadie. A sort of good luck charm, a kind of wishful thinking, as in, "Have faith. Keep good cheer. Things will work out in the end." But, like Sadie, they don't really believe in this stuff; they surely don't know it to be so—they just *sort* of, *kind* of, *hope* that things will work out.

And while many people "*frum* speak" and use the vernacular, they aren't any more sophisticated than Sadie—they just use different terms. "It's all *bashert*." "To succeed in life, you need *mazel*."

And it could well be that when they say, "It's *bashert*," they don't know the difference between *bitachon* or *mazel* or karma or voodoo or whatever. But it doesn't matter—because it's all the same. It's just some sort of, hazy, confused, wishful thinking.

This has nothing to do with *bitachon*. *Bitachon* is based on knowing that Hashem is active in the running of the world. *Bitachon* is founded on the knowledge that Hashem is with me throughout my day, observing, protecting, and helping me. *Bitachon* rests on the understanding that Hashem controls every outcome. It isn't *mazel*, and it isn't lucky rabbit feet—it's Hashem.

Before a person can reach any real level of *bitachon*, he has to have a firm grasp of the fourth level of *emunah*. He has to understand that Hashem is here. Right here. Active. Involved. Present and accounted for in the running of my life.

But there's one more point that requires understanding. Many times when people use the word *bitachon*, they mean "faith," as in, "We can't really know, but we have faith."

But faith and *bitachon* have very little to do with one another.

▶ Chapter Seventeen
I Have Faith in You

Faith is something that we have in people. Imagine that you offer to buy my car. You name a price, I agree, and then you ask, "Is it okay if I pay you by check?"

Hmmmm... Do I take your check or not? Well, it depends. If the amount is small, and I know you well, I probably have faith that you're good for the money. But if I'm selling my car for fifteen thousand dollars, and I don't know you that well, do I have faith that your check won't bounce?

If I'm selling my car for fifteen thousand dollars, and I don't know you that well, do I have faith that your check won't bounce?

Bitachon isn't supposed to be some sort of wistful, foggy "I hope it's true" sort of sense. It is **knowledge**. Knowing that Hashem is present. Knowing that Hashem isinvolved in my life. Knowing that Hashem will come through for me.

Once upon a time, there were people who had rock solid trust. The *Avos* were on that level. Avraham, Yitzchak, and Yaakov walked with Hashem. Sarah, Rivkah, Rachel, and Leah spoke to Hashem. Of course they trusted. Of course they weren't afraid. How could they be? Hashem was right there with them.

For us, our work lies in making our beliefs tangible. We have to come to see Hashem. We need to train ourselves to find Him. He's hiding, yet controlling all. We start with the big picture issues: by looking at the world and seeing that it has a Creator, studying the astonishing system of nature and getting a sense of awe of the One who formed it. Then we study life on this planet. We review history—the history of the world and the history of our lives. And then we discover Hashem. We see the Orchestrator behind the scenes, coordinating, choreographing all of the events of mankind's tumultuous existence. Eventually, we reach that goal of seeing Hashem. Not sort of hoping, or praying, or wishing—but *knowing* that Hashem is with us.

You may ask, "But how can a person know? If I can't see Hashem, can I truly know that He is here? Can I really know that He is active in my life?"

The answer to this is that there are many things we know even if we have never experienced them directly.

▶ Chapter Eighteen
Gravity and Emunah

Imagine that you're in a hotel room on the sixth floor, and you walk out onto the balcony overlooking the street. The scene below is breathtaking. The entire city is laid out in a panorama before you. To get an even better view, you lean over the railing a bit. Suddenly, a gust of wind pushes you from behind. You lose your balance. You totter — almost over the edge. In an instant, your eye spots the concrete below, and you realize this might be it. It might be all over.

Somehow, you grab the rail, regain your balance, and put your feet back on the balcony. By now your entire being is trembling. Your heart is racing. You are sweating.

"Oh, my gosh," you say to yourself. "I almost fell. I almost went crashing down. I could have died."

You slowly make your way back into the hotel room with a sense of being in another world.

Let's analyze this. As you were teetering over the edge, you didn't think that you might get hurt if you fell—you knew it. You knew it with absolute certainty. There was a clear understanding that falling forty-five feet to the concrete below would end very badly. That is knowledge. It isn't something that you sort of, kind of, want to believe. You *know* that gravity is real. You *know* that heavy objects fall and land with a thud.

▶ Emunah Is Knowledge

The Rambam defines the *mitzvah* of *emunah* as knowing Hashem. Not sort of hoping. Not faith. Not wishful thinking. *Knowing* Hashem. Having a real awareness of Hashem's presence. Hashem is right *here*, not thirteen billion light years up in the sky.

Even more than that is recognizing the fact that Hashem runs the world. Knowing in my bones that there is no activity on the planet that can occur without Hashem guiding it and directing it.

By studying the physical creation and its wonders, you see Hashem. By reflecting that Hashem is here, you begin to experience the awe of Hashem's presence, and your *emunah* reaches a whole new level.

However, the biggest change might well be in the way that you view other people. While they remain important, you now have a very different viewpoint of them, one that puts them into a new perspective.

▼

▶ Chapter Nineteen
You Can't Harm Me; You Can't Help Me

> *"Do not take revenge."*
>
> [*Vayikra* 19:18]
>
> *One day, you ask to borrow my shovel. I refuse. The next day, I say to you, "May I borrow your hammer?" You respond, "Yesterday, when I asked you for a shovel, you wouldn't help me. I'm going to pay you back in kind. Now that you need something, I won't help."*
>
> *This is an example of revenge.*
>
> [*Yoma* 23a]

The *Sefer HaChinuch* (241) explains that the Torah forbids us from taking revenge because everything that happens to us, good or bad, is directed by Hashem. No one can harm us without Hashem's will. Therefore, when someone causes us pain or suffering, we shouldn't seek to pay him back. We should recognize that the person isn't the cause of the damage. It has been directed to us by Hashem.

The *Sefer HaChinuch* is teaching us that if I take revenge, I am denying Hashem's involvement in my life. If Hashem runs the world, and everything comes from Him, why should I seek to hurt this man who "harmed" me? He is but the messenger. The misfortune was directed to me by my Creator.

By seeking revenge, I impute power to man. I am acknowledging that he can hurt me. That is a misunderstanding of the way that Hashem runs the world. I need to understand that it is Hashem alone Who controls my fate.

▶ You Can't Harm Me

This concept is one of the foundations of *bitachon:* understanding that Hashem decides what is best for me and decrees what will befall me. Things don't just happen. Nothing just occurs. Hashem decrees my fate, and nothing can change that. *"No person, animal, or other creation can harm me without Hashem's approval."* (Chovos HaLevovos, Sha'ar HaBitachon 3)

In simple terms, Hashem is there with me, 24/7, guiding my

If I take revenge, I am denying Hashem's involvement in my life.

life, protecting me, and nothing can touch me unless it is directed by Hashem. Stormy seas can't drown me. Hurricanes can't flood my home. Wild fires can't burn me. Drunk drivers can't kill me. Bears can't maul my children. No harm can befall me unless it was decreed by Hashem.

On its most practical level, this means that my fate is not in the hands of man. No human being can alter my state. If I was slated to be wealthy, you can't take that from me. If I was determined to enjoy honor, you can't defame me. If I wasn't supposed to suffer, you can't cause me pain.

You may dream and scheme, but Hashem is here, protecting me, guiding all outcomes. If I am to suffer, then it will happen regardless of your attempts. If it wasn't meant to be, nothing you do can change that. Every ounce of pain and suffering is weighed and meted out by Hashem. No one can alter that.

▶ I Walk Around in a Bubble

A way to relate to this is to imagine that you are surrounded by a plastic bubble. When you walk down the street, you can see out of the bubble. You can hear what's going on around you, but no one can reach in. They can try to throw rocks at you, but nothing will penetrate. They can try to hit you, but it won't happen. They can't touch you; you are shielded by the bubble. That bubble is comparable to Hashem. Hashem is protecting you. 24/7. 365. All day. Every day.

And this protection runs across the gamut of life. No one can cause you to lose a customer or a business deal. No one can cause you to be fired. No one can cause you to lose a *shidduch*. There may be people who wish for your harm, but they are powerless to change what Hashem has decreed. Hashem runs this world—not man. To illlustrate how far this concept extends, let me share an illustration.

▶ How to Take an Insult

When I was in third grade, I had a teacher who taught us how to accept a compliment. "Don't squirm," she would say. "Look the person in the eye, and say, 'Thank you.'"

While this was wise advice, I don't recall any teacher ever telling us how to take an insult. But the Chovos HaLevovos does: When someone insults you and causes you pain, you should turn your eyes heavenward and say, *"Thank You, Hashem, for revealing a few of my many flaws."* (*Shaar Bitachon* 3)

I must recognize that the words said by whoever insulted me were meant for me to hear. The one who spoke was a messenger sent by Hashem.

Looking at life from this perspective is transformative. People shrink down to size. Hurtful words lose their sting. I get it: it all comes from Hashem. Obviously, I don't get angry. How could I get angry? You didn't hurt me; you didn't insult me—you are just the puppet mouthing the words. There was Someone behind the scenes, pulling the strings.

As a parable:

▶ Punching the Loudspeaker

Imagine that I am speaking to a large audience, and because of the size of the crowd, I am using a microphone. I go through my presentation point by point, and then suddenly I stop. I stare directly at you. Then, I turn red in the face, point my finger at you, and start yelling: "You are a good-for-nothing, lowly, worthless bum. I didn't know such foul people even exist!" And I proceed to call you every name in the book.

How would you react? I would imagine that you would be incensed. "I can't believe he did that!" you might say to yourself. "He insulted me. He ripped me to shreds—in public, no less. What right did he have to do that?"

Now imagine that you get so angry, you decide to take matters into your own hands. You stand up, walk over to the loudspeaker, and smash your fist right into the subwoofer.

That would be a foolish reaction. If you were to punch me, we could debate whether that's clever. But punching the loudspeaker doesn't make any sense. The loudspeaker didn't insult you. I did.

That is what the Chovos HaLevovos is teaching us. No man can harm me. If you yell at me, if you call me names, if you embarrass me—I am supposed to understand that those words are meant for me to hear. They are being directed from Hashem right to me. You are nothing but the loudspeaker. So I am supposed to turn my eyes heavenward, acknowledge the source of the message, and say, "Thank You, Hashem, for revealing a few of my many flaws."

▶ No One Can Help You Either

But there is also a flip side. No one can help me either.

If I were destined to struggle financially, the wealthiest man in the world can't change that decree. If I was slated to be sick, my uncle could be the head of Oncology at Sloan Kettering Hospital, but there'll be nothing that he can do for me. Hashem metes out pain and suffering in a very measured and defined manner—and no one can interfere.

People don't make me rich. Connections don't help me get ahead. My business acumen doesn't make me wealthy. If I am supposed to get that money, it will come from this pipeline or from that one. If I'm not supposed to have that money, it may come in for a while, but I will eventually lose it. No one can change Hashem's decree. Across the full spectrum of the human experience, Hashem is directly and intimately involved in the running of our lives.

This concept forces us to rethink the power given to man and our entire understanding of the concept of free will.

▶ Chapter Twenty

Outcomes and Intentions

Imagine that Reuven walks up to Shimon, pulls out a gun and says, "I'm going to kill you!"

"No, no! Don't do it!" shouts Shimon.

Reuven responds, "You have this coming to you!"

He then fires five shots, leaving Shimon dead in a puddle of blood.

If the Jewish high court, the *Sanhedrin*, were in existence, and there was sufficient evidence, they would convict Reuven as the killer of Shimon.

Here is the question. Why can't Reuven tell the *Sanhedrin*, "Aren't you religious Jews? Don't you believe that Hashem decrees who will live and who will die? If you do, then I'm not Reuven's killer—Hashem is. If it wasn't slated to happen, I could never have done it. So don't go blaming me."

Why isn't his claim valid?

The answer is that on one level, his claim is a hundred percent correct. If Shimon wasn't slated to die, there is nothing that Reuven could have done to harm him. But to allow for free will, Hashem created a system where man is held accountable for what he does.

If, on the previous Rosh Hashanah, Shimon was decreed a year of life, then there is nothing that Reuven or any other force in existence could do to change that.

If, however, it was decreed that this would be Shimon's last year in this world, then things get more complicated. There are times when Hashem will allow another person the "opportunity" to be the messenger. If Shimon were decreed to die that year in a violent manner, Hashem might also decree that certain individuals have the option of becoming the one to end his life. In that case, Reuven might be granted the opportunity to kill Shimon. If Reuven doesn't take that option, then Shimon will be hit by a drunk driver, a falling telephone pole, a stray bullet, or any number of other death-causing events.

But if Reuven does take this option, then he is called the "killer" of Shimon—even though it's true that this decree was decided by Hashem long ago and that Shimon would have died anyway. To allow for free will, Hashem gives man certain options, and if he takes those options, the act is attributed to him. For all intents and purposes, he is considered the one who did the act—certainly in terms of all of man's dealings.

The underlying concept is that man is in charge of his *inten-*

tions; Hashem is in charge of the *outcome*. Hashem gives the illusion that one man can change the destiny of another. If man opts on that illusion, then the act is attributed to him—even though the same consequence would have occurred without him.

▶ My Relationship to You

This perspective changes my relationships with other people in a rather dramatic form. If you try to help me, I am appreciative... for your intentions. You tried to help. That part—the attempt—is in your hands. You tried to lighten my load, and for that I am thankful. But the result, whether you succeed or not, is not in your hands.

If someone saves my life, I have to thank him for his good intentions. I have to recognize that he desired to help me, and for that I have to be appreciative. At the same time, I recognize that he was but fulfilling Hashem's decree. If he would not have been there, a speed boat would have pulled up or a floating log would have suddenly passed by or some other kind of messenger would have suddenly appeared to save me. While he is credited as being the one who saved me and I have to be appreciative of his good intentions, I also have to recognize that that same result would have happened without him as well. The one who saved me wasn't him—it was Hashem.

> *You tried to lighten my load, and for that I am thankful. But the result, whether you succeed or not, is not in your hands.*

If I needed money and someone gave me a large sum, I have to be thankful for his good wishes and his desire to help me. But I have to be mindful that if not for him, that money would have come to me through other means.

If you attempt to harm me, this concept tempers my attitude as well. I didn't ask you to be the nudnik to bring this about, but I understand that it would have happened, with or without you. So my anger at you is greatly diminished. For wishing me harm, I have my issues with you. But for bringing it about, not at all. The results have nothing to do with you.

Man controls intentions; Hashem controls outcomes.

This is what the *Sefer HaChinuch* is teaching us. The only reason I would seek revenge is because *you* hurt me, *you* wronged me, *you* took something from me. If I recognize that Hashem alone determines every outcome, I would never get angry. I might feel disappointment that you have chosen poorly, but anger only comes from the sense that you have *done* something to me. And that sense is illusory.

Chapter Twenty-One
Understanding the Decree

And now we come to the core issue of *bitachon*.

The Chovos HaLevovos describes that *bitachon* is based on the understanding that my financial status, my health and well-being, which woman I am to marry, which home I am to own, and countless other life circumstances have been decided by Hashem—and there is nothing that anyone can do to change that.

Hashem created me and put me into a life. That life was carefully planned to allow me to reach my potential. All of the props on the stage of my life have been set. I didn't choose my level of intelligence, my personality, or my temperament. I wasn't asked to pick the family I would be born into, nor the generation in which I would live. These were all hand-picked by my Creator to give me the perfect challenge to allow me to reach the greatness that I am able to achieve.

Just as my nature and physical stature has been chosen for me, the other settings of my life have also been predetermined. My role is to go out and use the world as Hashem wants me to. In order to earn a living, I have to work hard. When it's time to get married, I have to search for my spouse. When I'm sick, I have to find a doctor. But not just any doctor—the most competent medical professional I can find. I have to go through the motions. And all the while, I have to understand that I am doing just that—*going through the motions*. Hashem has determined what is for my best, and that is exactly what will come about. I have to do my part by using this world in the ways of the world. Once I do that, Hashem will bring about that which He has deemed to be for my best.

This is the first step in *bitachon:* recognizing that Hashem decrees my fate. For these concepts to affect my thoughts and feelings, they have to become firmly embedded in my mind; they have to become real. To do that, I have to train myself to view reality from a higher perspective. I have to see Hashem as active in my world.

But even after I've spent much time focusing, thinking, and growing in these areas, I still have to learn to *trust* Hashem. To do that, there are two concepts that must become clear.

> Chapter Twenty-Two
Hashem Loves You

Recently, I was speaking in an out-of-town community on the topic of the four levels of *emunah*. I spent some time dwelling on the third level: that Hashem knows our thoughts. I explained the parable of the transparent man: that Hashem peers into my essence and knows exactly what I'm thinking as I think it. When I was finished, a number of people came up to ask questions. I also noticed two young women hovering on the side waiting. When everyone else left, they came over to me, and one said in a very agitated voice: "This is terrible! How can I live with this?"

"What do you mean?" I asked.

"I mean this idea that Hashem knows my inner thoughts. I feel so exposed. How can I live with that knowledge?"

Her friend explained that she was a *ba'alas teshuvah*, and that she had been brought up by an abusive father. The idea of someone knowing her inner thoughts was very threatening to her.

I tried to gently explain that she was being anthropomorphic, projecting human characteristics onto Hashem. She was comparing Hashem to the people in her life. And you can't compare Hashem to men or women or anyone else. Hashem is miles and miles above any human limitation.

"Naturally," I said, "if you view Hashem as a human, then there are many things that you will find troubling. But that's the point—Hashem isn't human."

I went on to explain that Hashem is limitless and boundless, contained neither by space nor by time. Hashem is all-knowing and all-powerful. For us to even discuss Hashem in any meaningful way requires us to break out of our limited experiences.

"One of the reasons that we find it so difficult to relate to Hashem," I continued, "is that His very essence contradicts all that we experience. In our world, everything is limited; everything has a beginning and an end. Trees are a hundred feet tall. Bulls weigh two thousand pounds. A dog lives for ten years. Everything we know can be weighed and measured—they are so wide, so heavy, and so tall—because they are contained by limitations. But Hashem has no limitations. So, by definition, for us to comprehend Hashem on any level, we need to step outside of our frame of reference."

While I could see that she understood where I was headed, she was still troubled. So I said to her, "I would like to ask you a question."

▶ Chapter Twenty-Three

What Did You Do to Be Worthy of Being Created?

"Before you were created," I said, "what did you do to be worthy of being created?"

"What do you mean?"

"I mean, at some point you didn't exist. Then Hashem decided to create you. Before you were created, what did you do that made Hashem say, 'Such an individual is worthy for Me to create.'

"The answer is—nothing. Before you were created, you didn't exist. You couldn't do anything to be worthy of being created... because you weren't.

"It may sound obvious, but it is really profound. Hashem created you for one reason—to give to you. Hashem is magnanimous, loving, and kind. Hashem wants to share of His good. Hashem made you—not because you were worthy, not because of anything that you did, nor because of anything that you will do. Hashem made you for one reason: to give to you.

"And there is nothing that Hashem needs in return," I went on. "Hashem lacks nothing—so there is nothing that you could ever do for Him. The sole reason that Hashem made you was to share of His good with you.

"So the very first point that you need to understand in your connection with Hashem is that it's a one-way relationship. Hashem is the giver and you are the receiver."

I saw that I had her thinking, but we still had a way to go. So I pressed forward. "There's a second question," I said, "that is equally important to ask yourself."

▶ Chapter Twenty-Four

What Can You Do to Make Hashem Angry?

"The second question is: what can you do to make Hashem angry?

"Let's say that one day you decide, 'That's it. I'm fed up with Hashem, and I'm going to do something to get Him angry.' What could you do to make Hashem really mad?

"The answer is nothing. Because, quite frankly, you're not important enough to make Hashem angry.

"Hashem is the Creator of all. Hashem said, 'It should be,' and everything—energy, matter, quarks, atoms, and molecules—came into being. Hashem is also the Maintainer of physicality. Nothing can exist without Hashem constantly infusing energy into it.

"If Hashem ever got angry, He wouldn't need to zap a person. He wouldn't need to bring about a nuclear holocaust. Hashem would simply stop imparting energy into that person, and he would cease to be. So Hashem doesn't need to get angry."

▶ Hashem Can't Get Angry

But more accurately, Hashem can't get angry. By definition, anything physical is confined. Because we are corporeal, we exist for a given amount of time. We take up a given amount of space. We can run just so fast, walk just so far. Hashem is beyond all boundaries and beyond all confines. Hashem is in all places at all times, existing before and after time. Hashem is so above all of nature that there is nothing that is beyond His powers. There's nothing that He can't do.

The reason I get angry is because I'm frustrated by my lack of power and control. But nothing is beyond Hashem; nothing is out of His control. Therefore, anger doesn't apply to Him.

When Hashem gives free will to man, He gives us the ability to make choices—but He governs the outcome. We control our intentions; Hashem controls the results. If man chooses evil, there are times when Hashem will allow those actions to come to fruition. And there are times when He will not. That is up to His ultimate wisdom. Either way, when man chooses to do evil, he damages himself. Hashem is the Master of the Universe. He will either let that action come to bear fruit or He will prevent it. But at no point is

> *Hashem is so above all of nature that there is nothing that is beyond His powers. There's nothing that He can't do.*

Hashem not in control. So the concept of Hashem being angry is philosophically impossible. Hashem can't get angry.

Hashem only wants what's good for His creations, and therefore, so to speak, He can be saddened or disappointed. But the notion of Hashem being angry stems from a lack of comprehending His greatness.

"To gain a mature appreciation of our Creator, we need to understand that just as Hashem doesn't need us and doesn't gain from us, Hashem doesn't get angry with us."

At this point, I could almost see this young woman's mood lift as these ideas settled in. So I went on, "If you want to fully understand your relationship with Hashem, there is a third question that you need to ask yourself."

▶ Chapter Twenty-Six

Hashem Loves You More than You Love Yourself

The Chovos HaLevovos explains that in order to have *bitachon,* you must realize that Hashem cares about you in a very real way. You must appreciate that Hashem is deeply concerned for your good. And you must know that Hashem loves you.

But Hashem doesn't care about you as a mortal cares about you. Hashem looks out for your best interests, but not as a friend or a loved one might. Hashem looks out for your well-being immeasurably more than you or anyone else ever could. And most significantly, Hashem loves you—but not as a person loves another person. Hashem loves you more than anyone could ever love you. *Hashem loves you infinitely more than you love yourself.*

▼

But this greatly understates the concept. When we say that Hashem loves us more than any other person does, we are still thinking of Hashem in human terms. This is so limiting to Hashem that it is in the category of being insulting.

To put this into the proper light, Chazal use a parable. Imagine that long ago, two peasants were discussing the wealth of the king. "Why, the king is so wealthy," said the first peasant, "that he probably has a hundred silver coins."

"What?!" countered the second peasant. "A hundred silver coins? Why, I bet the king is so rich that he has more than a hundred *gold* coins!"

Both simpletons are insulting to the king. The king's wealth isn't measured in numbers of silver or gold coins. The king's treasure houses are filled with diamonds and pearls, precious metals and rubies; he owns vaults and vaults of gold and silver bars. Because the peasants are so small in their thinking, their attempt to praise the king is actually an insult to him.

In the same vein, any attempt to paint Hashem's concern for His creations in human terms is myopic. Physical beings have limits—Hashem doesn't. If Hashem cares about someone, it is limitless—without borders and confines. And if Hashem loves someone, that love breaks all boundaries and parameters.

> **When we say that Hashem loves us more than any other person does, we are still thinking of Hashem in human terms.**

If you were to take the most giving, loving individual you have ever known, and multiply that love by ten thousand, you wouldn't even begin to understand the love that Hashem has for any of His Creations.

This is the foundation of *bitachon:* knowing that Hashem loves you and that He is looking out for your good. Without it, trusting in Hashem is foolish. How can I rely on Hashem if He doesn't care about me? How can I trust in Hashem if I am of no importance to Him? The only way that a person can develop a sense of confidence in his Creator is by understanding that Hashem loves him to an extent that is beyond human comprehension.

If we understood the extent of Hashem's love for us, we would feel a tremendous sense of trust and reliance on Him. If Hashem is that concerned for my good, then of course I can trust that He will do everything possible to help me.

▶ Growing in Bitachon

The problem, however, is that these concepts are hard to feel. It is hard for us to imagine the unlimited; it is difficult for us to visualize something without bounds. It is too distant from our reality. Therefore, to help us grow in *bitachon*, it is wise to use examples from our frame of reference.

For example:

▶ Abba, Please Make Them Stop!

When my son was five years old, he was running a high fever and complained that his leg was hurting. I took him to the pediatrician, who examined him and ordered blood tests and an X-ray. It turned out that the little guy was running a 105° fever and had a broken leg. Not good signs—the doctor feared the worst. He immediately sent us to the emergency room; we had to find out what was going on.

At the hospital, they put him through more exams and more blood tests, but still nothing was conclusive. The attending physician told me that the only way he could rule out a life-threatening disease was to draw a blood sample from a vein deep in the thigh. I agreed to the procedure, and he asked us to wait in one of the emergency operating rooms.

By this time, it was already late at night and my son was very tired. When the two tall technicians, wearing gowns and masks, walked in to draw blood, I don't think he was quite ready for them. But it got worse. One of these "masked men" asked me to help hold the patient down. When we had him firmly in position, the other technician pulled out a LOOOOONG needle, which he directed toward the inside of my son's thigh.

At that point, my son looked up at me, and with terror in his voice pleaded, "Abba, make them stop! Please! Make them stop!"

My heart melted. What could I say? We had to do this. So I steeled myself and looked the other way.

Baruch Hashem, the results of the blood test were negative, and we went home with a diagnosis of a broken leg and a simple virus.

▶ A Father Feels His Son's Pain

The Chovos HaLevovos explains that a father feels his son's pain like his own. A father views his son as an extension of himself. So it's not his son's arm that's being cut; it's his own.

We recognize this as parental instinct. But where does that instinct come from? Why do parents feel such a powerful connection to their children? Why are parents willing to give up their lives for their children?

Hashem wants children to be loved and cared for, so He created this instinct and implanted into the heart of man, a sense of devotion to their offspring.

In plain language, any mercy that a child experiences came about because Hashem created those sentiments. When I was a young boy and stepped on a nail, I went running to my mother. The reason she gathered me in her arms and comforted me was that Hashem wanted me to feel secure. When I cut my arm and cried out in horror, "All of my blood is spilling out!" my father scooped me up and calmed me down because Hashem wanted me to be cared for. Any kindness or love that I have ever experienced was created by Hashem.

▶ Finding Favor in People's Eyes

This concept goes even deeper. Did you ever find that in one setting you were warmly accepted and in another you weren't? Do you remember being popular in one social environment while in a similar one, you were almost an outcast? And it's not that you changed, and not that the people were so different. It's just that sometimes you find favor in people's eyes, and sometimes you don't.

The Chovos HaLevovos explains that any time that people look at you favorably, it's because Hashem is there on the scene influencing them. If you are accepted and warmly received, it is because Hashem wills that to be. The reason your parents didn't tire of you after six months of getting up in the middle of night for you, changing you, and putting up with your colicky crying is that Hashem was there warming their hearts. The reason that your fourth grade teacher took a special interest in you was because Hashem was concerned for you.

In short, any kindness or love that you have received from another person was brought about by Hashem.

▶ Looking Back on Your Life

This concept is huge. Think back over your life. Any time someone did you a favor, any time someone had mercy on you, any time someone showed you kindness—it was because Hashem caused that person to feel a sense of love toward you.

Just as when you were four years old and woke up in the middle of the night crying from a nightmare, and your mother was there to comfort you—in every situation throughout your life, no matter how big or little, Hashem was there directing your care.

▶ Putting This into Practice

While this concept may sound lofty, one of the ways to put it into practice is to look at your own life. Every Jew has a story. If you look back at the things that have happened to you, the people you just happened to meet, the situations that just happened to unfold—you start seeing a pattern. You begin recognizing that Hashem was there, helping, protecting, and guiding you. At the time, you might

In every situation throughout your life, no matter how big or little, Hashem was there directing your care.

have thought you were alone. Now, in retrospect, it's clear—Hashem was doing all that for your good.

It's a good idea to write down these events of your life as they occur. Whenever a strange or significant event happens, and you excitedly say the words, *"Baruch Hashem,* it's such *hashgachah!"* that's the time to write it down.

After a year, when you go back and read through your entries, you will begin to see the tapestry. And it's not "in theory" or in a book about great people living long ago. It's your life, and it's real. Then you will experience a powerful recognition. "Look! Hashem was there. And there. And there as well. Wow! Hashem cares about me. Hashem is in my life. Hashem loves me."

So while the first condition for *bitachon*—knowing that Hashem is more concerned about my good than I am—may sound removed, it isn't that difficult to work on. It is the second condition, however, that creates untold amounts of trouble for most people.

▶ Chapter Twenty-Seven

How Smart Is Hashem?

▶ I Heard a Rustling

It was late Friday night. I was walking to a friend's house when I heard a rustling in the bushes. I looked over, and in the shrubs I saw it—a rat. I can't say I jumped. I can't say I ran. It was like being zapped with an electric shock. I found myself fifteen feet away, in the middle of the street, with my heart pounding and pulse racing.

What I experienced was the fight or flight response. When in danger, our bodies switch into emergency mode, and we get a surge of energy that allows us to perform acts of strength well beyond our normal limits. The stories are legendary: A fireman lifts a burning beam that supports an entire wall. A climber trapped under a twelve hundred pound rock shoves the rock down an embankment. A mother lifts a car, freeing her trapped child. Feats of strength that under normal circumstances would be impossible.

While we recognize the adrenaline rush that brings on this state, the actual process is astonishingly complex. To appreciate it, let's take a moment to look at the body.

▶ The Human Body

On a mechanical level, the body is a set of interacting machines. Each organ is a part of a system; each system is linked to other systems. The heart is the pump, delivering nutrients to the cells. The liver is the food manufacturer, creating glucose—fuel to power the muscles. The kidneys are the filters, removing waste products. The lungs are the air movers, bringing in oxygen and transporting it to the blood. The muscles are the engines that do everything from aiding in digestion to lifting your arms, legs, head, and chest.

Because each organ has a specific role and functions in a particular manner, there must be an overall guidance system to regulate it. For instance, the heart beats 100,000 times a day. What tells it how often to pump, how hard to pump, and at what rhythm? Glucose is a highly specific chemical formula. What tells the liver the appropriate chemical composition? What tells it where to store the glucose and how to release it? What tells the lungs how deeply to breathe and at what rate? What tells the muscles the order in which to squeeze and contract so that the diaphragm will lift and rise?

The answer is that a specific area of the brain regulates each organ. Intricate nerve pathways signal the release of chemicals that control the balance and function of each structure. The neuroscience and biochemistry of all these systems and functions are so complex, they can fill libraries.

▶ Systems Dependent upon Systems

And things are even more complicated because each system is dependent upon other systems for its functioning. The brain can't function unless the heart provides it with blood, and the heart can't function unless it is supplied with oxygen by the lungs. The kidneys can't filter unless the liver supplies them with fuel, and the liver can't provide fuel if the digestive tract doesn't break down food. And all of these are dependent upon the circulatory system to deliver nutrients and remove waste.

Each organ alone requires numerous steps and hundreds of different chemicals to ensure its proper functioning. Each of those steps is made up of dozens and dozens of sub-steps and cascades of chemical reactions. To keep all the systems and organs functioning in balance requires processing more complex than any computer that man has ever designed.

▶ Understanding the Fight or Flight Response

Because the fight or flight response engages almost every organ and system in the body, the complexity of this operation is especially baffling.

At the first hint of danger, early warning signals are sent to the fear center in the brain, the amygdala, via the optic nerve. This prepares the body for action. If the danger is confirmed, the disaster center in the brain jumpstarts the body. Nerve impulses are fired down the spinal cord to the adrenal glands just above the kidneys. The glands flood the blood stream with adrenaline, which boosts heart rate and blood pressure. Blood now races to the muscles. Adrenaline also signals the liver to flood the body with glucose—blood sugar—for fuel. Blood is shunted away from the digestive tract and other non-vital areas to allow for more blood in critical areas. The lungs are signaled to breathe more quickly and deeply, thereby injecting more oxygen into the blood. The metabolism is quickened. All senses are on high alert. The mind is hyperfocused. The body is primed—ready to lift, run, or fight.

▶ ATP — Emergency Fuel for Muscles

But this isn't enough. In life and death situations, every millisecond counts, and the body must respond immediately. What kickstarts that sprint to safety or the powerful lunge into battle, is instant energy stored in the muscles.

Long in advance of an emergency situation, the body stockpiles energy—much like a high-energy battery—in the form of ATP, an energy molecule produced when glucose or fat is burned. An emergency supply of ATP is housed in the muscles, ready to turbo charge us on demand. For a few seconds, that energy burst can turn a middle-aged man into an Olympic sprinter,

All senses are on high alert. The mind is hyperfocused. The body is primed—ready to lift, run, or fight.

or a housewife into a power lifter. The supply only lasts about four seconds, and then it's consumed. But during that time, we are able to perform superhuman feats of strength—pushing the body well beyond its limits.

The dazzling part is that it's automatic. It usually happens before our conscious mind even recognizes the danger. One minute you are calmly walking down the street. Then, suddenly, the eyes see, the brain responds, and within a flash, mild-mannered Clark Kent is transformed into Superman—ready to save the day.

But if we look into this even further, we will see there is a lot more going on behind the scenes.

▶ Looking into Eyesight

If you think of an object—say a pen—your brain retrieves its name, its shape, its function, and even the sound it makes when it scratches across paper. Each part of this memory comes from a different region of the brain, and so when you think of a pen, its entire image is being actively reconstructed by the brain from information stored in many different areas. Neurologists are only beginning to understand how the parts are reassembled into a coherent whole. But it is a fantastically complex process.

We normally think of our senses in simplistic terms. We see. We hear. We feel. We taste. But what's actually going on is far more than just that. Our mind is taking in sensory input and processing it—making sense of what it is that we are experiencing. Our brain decodes, assembles, and then compares images that have accumulated over the span of a lifetime to bring us a coherent version of what is happening. The steps involved in the process are remarkable.

Let's take vision for instance. When I looked at the bushes and saw that rat, what actually happened?

I heard a rustling sound and turned my head to see what it was. As I turned to look, the lens in my eye automatically adjusted to focus on an image. That image was projected onto the retina in the back of my eye. Cells in the retina converted that image into electrical impulses, which were sent along the optic nerve into my brain for decoding and deciphering, the question being: "What is that object? Is it real? Is it a threat?"

Next began the process of perception. Every second, a billion items of information are sent through the eye. Initially, everything that enters is a blur with an untold number of patches of light and dark, contours and lines. Information is then sent to different regions of the brain to piece together the image, refocus the eye for greater detail, and then interpret what it is that I am looking at. To do this, the supercomputer we call the brain must go into high gear.

▶ The Visual Cortex

The first stop is the thalamus. The raw information is brought here, and the first stages of recognition happen. Here the brain begins to gather and interpret the data, reaching some initial composites.

"Let's see... that object is furry, has big ears, and a tail. Hmmmmm... What could it be? Mickey Mouse has big ears and a tail... No, that can't be it. He isn't furry. Well, a cat is furry and has a tail... No, a cat doesn't have ears like that... Hmmmm. I wonder what this is?"

A signal is now sent to the visual cortex. "We need help

identifying this. It's clearly an animal, but what kind? Is it friendly or predatory?"

Signals are then relayed to the memory center to access previous visual images. Every image a person sees is burnt into a cell. These cells are inventoried by category, emotion, and feelings. The catalogue of these cells is consulted to make a connection. Picture after picture is accessed until some recognitions form.

"Ah, look there's my pet hamster I owned when I was ten. Nope. Not him. What about this? It's furry and has a tail. No, that's a dog... Hey, what about this? Yeah. That looks right. I think that's it. Yeah. But, hey, wait, that's a... a... a RAT!"

Since the visual image of a rat was stored with severe emotions attached, the message comes back with a red flag, as in: "Watch out! This might be dangerous!"

▶ Context

But not all rats are a threat. It depends on a number of factors. Is the rat close by? Is it caged? Is it real? If I'm standing in the zoo, and the rat is behind a two-inch thick piece of glass, I am not in harm's way. More information is needed.

So signals are sent to the hippocampus to determine context. "Where am I? Where's the rat? What are the circumstances?"

Every image a person sees is burnt into a cell. These cells are inventoried by category, emotion, and feelings.

The answer comes back. "I am standing alone on a dark street, late at night. Not good."

Now the major number crunching part takes place—putting it all together. The message comes in from the memory center: "Rat! Rat! Rat! This is not a drill! I repeat, this is not a drill!"

The context center relays the word: "We are in a situation—without backup."

The thalamus then puts it all together. "Rat. Night. Alone. TROUBLE! Immediate action is required!"

It then fires off a signal to the crisis center of the brain: "Warning. Warning. Red Alert. Danger."

The amygdala, the area that controls strong emotions, is signaled. It shoots a message to the hypothalamus, which then fires electrical impulses down the spine to the adrenal gland. Thirty hormones are released, sending commands to almost every system in the body. The heart and lungs are sent into overdrive. The brain is flooded with chemicals that focus attention. The pupils are dilated to allow in more light. The veins in the skin constrict to force more blood to the muscles—causing the familiar sensation of goose bumps. The immune and digestive system are shut down to allow more energy to the muscles. The liver secretes glucose and begins production of replenishments. ATP in the muscles is released—and the body is ready for peak performance.

From start to finish how long does the complete process take?

About 3/10th of a second.

We are looking at a system of extreme complexity. It's more sophisticated than the finest machines, systems, or factories that man has ever conceived. But even at this level, we're only scratching the surface of what is happening. To appreciate the complexity of this response, we need to take a step back.

▶ Parlor Trick

Ask a smart eight-year-old the following riddle: Here's a choice. Either I will give you a million dollars now, or I will give you a penny today, double it tomorrow, and double the amount you have each day for thirty days. Which would you choose?

Any self-respecting third grader would, of course, go for the million dollars. A million dollars is a huge sum.

That third grader, however, would have chosen poorly. Because if you take a penny and double it, then take those two pennies and double them, and keep doubling that amount, the base number that you are multiplying gets larger and larger so that the product increases exponentially. And two to the thirtieth power equals 1.073 billion!

▶ How the Brain Works

This concept is critical to understanding how the brain works. All brain activity is made up of neurons communicating with each other. A neuron is a tiny cell that acts both as a receiver and transmitter of messages. When a neuron receives a message, it passes it along to one of its neighbors via chemical signals. Those chemicals cause the next receiving neuron to fire off an electrical impulse. One neuron signals the next. That neuron then signals the one after. That one signals the next, and onwards until the final destination is reached. All communication is made up of transferring these signals from neuron to neuron along established pathways.

Here is the interesting part.

Each neuron has a number of endings through which it transmits and receives signals from its neighbors. A neuron looks almost like a tadpole with tentacles or branches. Each transmitting neuron has many branches from which to send the signal. Each receiving neuron likewise has many branches with which to receive the signal. Which branch receives the message makes all the difference in what the signal means, what part of the brain to send it to, and what to do after that. And this is where things get complicated.

Since the transmitting neuron has many branches, it could send a signal through branch A, B, C, D, E, or F. The receptor neuron, as well, has many branches, and could receive the signal by branch W, X, Y, or Z. Since each neuron is in close proximity to many other neurons, it turns out that there are many, many paths through which a signal could be sent.

Let's think about this. If the brain were made up of only thirty neurons with thirty branches each, the possible pathways that a signal could follow would be thirty to the thirtieth power, a huge number. But the brain isn't made up of thirty neurons. A pinpoint of the visual cortex contains up to thirty thousand neurons! Each of those neurons can communicate with up to fifty thousand other neurons. So the possible pathways aren't thirty to the thirtieth power. It is thirty thousand to the fifty thousandth power! A number so large that it is inconceivable.

But of course there's more to the brain than the visual cortex—a lot more. There's the amygdala, the hypothalamus, the hippocampus, the neo-cortex. The brain is made up of a hundred billion neurons, each with as many as fifty thousand connections. The math works out to be a hundred billion to the fifty thousandth power—a number so astronomical that it defies human comprehension.

▼

▶ The Question

Here is the question: how does the signal know to go from this neuron to that one? And from that one to that one? The possibilities are so vast, and the paths so winding, convoluted, and complex, how does it know to follow this particular intricate conduit?

This question has baffled men of science for decades.

By far the most complex item in the known universe is the human brain.

Why is this significant to us? Because by studying the creation, we can gain an eye glimpse to the Creator. When we contemplate such wisdom, we begin to get an inkling of the sheer brilliance and capacity of Hashem. And for a person to trust Hashem, he must have a very clear understanding that Hashem's wisdom is so far beyond man that there is no basis for comparison. Anyone who does not understand this will fall prey to the one common mistake that has plagued man for centuries.

► Chapter Twenty-Eight

Stop Playing God

Eighty percent of our *emunah* problems and ninety percent of our questions on Hashem stem from one mistake—we play God. Playing God means I know exactly what I need. I need to marry *that* woman. I need *that* job. I need my child to get into *that* school.

I've talked to Hashem about it. I've explained it to Him. I've even brokered deals with Him. "If You grant me this, I'll..."

Yet for some reason, He just won't listen.

"Hashem, what's the deal? Are You angry with me? Are You punishing me? Why do You insist on making my life so difficult? This is what I need. Why won't You just listen to me?"

And I go on asking questions. "It's not fair. It doesn't make sense! Hashem, what do You want from me?"

The problem here is quite simple—I am playing God. And I'm not God. The simple reality is that *maybe*, just *maybe*, it's not going because it's not *supposed* to go. Maybe Hashem knows better than I do what is for my best. "Hmmmm... I never thought about that..."

▶ Historical Perspective

This is peculiar because I've lived through situations that didn't turn out as I thought they would. I absolutely had to have that job; it was just what I needed. I could earn a living, support my family, and still have time to learn. It was the perfect fit. In the end, I didn't get the job, and I had major questions. "Hashem, why?! Why aren't You there for me?" Then, five years later, I find out that the entire industry is being shipped over to India. Oh...

A different time, I tried to marry that woman. She was perfect; great match, good family. She would make a fantastic wife and mother for my children. And it didn't go. "Hashem, why have you abandoned me? This is what I need!" She ended up marrying someone else. Then, two years later, I find out that the term "mentally unstable" is a mild description of her situation. Mmmmm...

Then it was my son. My son absolutely, positively, had to get into that class; it was just what he needed. Great *rebbe*, good atmosphere—it was perfect. And the

The problem here is quite simple—I am playing God. And I'm not God.

menahel wouldn't let. "Hashem, why? Where are You?" Then, two months later, I found out that there's a child in that class who would have been the worst possible influence on my son. It would have been devastating. Hmmmm...

▶ Part of Human Nature

The ironic part is that we do this all the time. We act as if we truly know what is best for us. We run after it. We hotly pursue it.

"No obstacle will stand in *my* way. Nothing will prevent *this* from coming about."

And when lo and behold, my efforts are thwarted—the questions begin. "But, why? It's not fair! I am a good person. Hashem, why won't You just help me?"

It's easy to see the folly of this when other people do it, but when it happens in my world, then the real challenge begins. To break out of this, we need to change perspective.

▶ Hashem Knows Better than I Do What Is for My Best

The concept we need to embrace is that *Hashem knows better than I do what is best for me.* As smart as I may be, and as clear as it is to me that this is what I need, Hashem still knows better. That is the second condition of *bitachon.*

In theory, this should be easy to see. After all, how much do I know? How far into the future can I really see? But the problem isn't in the world of theory. The problem is in my world—in the thick and thin of life.

It's when I know so clearly that this is what I need and it's not happening that the challenge begins. So I go back and forth in my mind. "Yes, I would like to trust Hashem, but... how can I possibly believe that Hashem is doing this for my good? I know it's not true. You can't ask me to accept something I know is false. If I weren't sure, it would be one thing, but this is so clear and so obvious. I know what I need."

▶ The Solution: The Bigger Picture

The solution is to put some perspective into my thinking. Often it requires talking to myself, having actual conversations in my mind where I challenge myself.

"Let's see... Who should I trust—myself or Hashem? Well, let's do the math. Who am I? Who is Hashem?

"Hashem created the heavens and the earth and all that they contain. He wrote the formulas for quantum physics and molecular biology. He views the entire universe with one glance. He sees the future as the past. And He has the wisdom to see far-reaching results. What will this bring to ten years from now? What will the consequences be twenty years from now?

"I, on the other hand, see about two inches in front of my face. I make mistakes. I get confused and caught up. I forget. I forget lessons. I forget facts. I forget consequences. I can't remember what I had for breakfast this morning. And as much as I think I know, I am often wrong. That which I think will be so good for me, so many times isn't.

"Hashem, on the other hand, remembers every event since Creation. Hashem sees from one end of history to the other. And Hashem made me. He is my Creator, and *He knows me even better than I do, so He understands my needs better than I do.*

"Who do I think has it right? Me or Hashem? Me or Hashem? Mmmmm. Let me get back to you on that one."

▶ The Brick Wall

While this may sound ludicrous—it is—until, in the busyness of doing and going and accomplishing, this simple reality fades from my sight. I start going through the routine of: "I need that. I must have this. I have to accomplish that." And when I face the brick wall blocking my path, I push on, bucking against everything in front of me. And I ask questions: "Hashem, where are You? Why aren't You helping me?"

▶ The Ultimate Challenge

The reason this is such a challenge is that I am obligated to use this world as Hashem wants me to, which means I have to engage my best effort. I have to use my wisdom, ask advice, plan, and think. When I do, there is a natural consequence that I start reaching conclusions. This is what I need. This is what's best. This is what should happen.

The great challenge of life is to be actively engaged in the ways of the world, but at the same time remember that it is Hashem's world. He is the Master, and He alone controls all outcomes. I have to trust that His decisions are for my best.

And so it takes constant vigilance, a constant monitoring of our thoughts and asking ourselves, "Is my thinking in line with my beliefs? What if someone else presented this situation to me? What would I say to them?" Interestingly, most of the time, when the question is framed that way, the answer is obvious.

When a person has full *bitachon*, there is a beautiful calm that settles over him. It's not that life now is all rosy, peaches and cream—it's that he understands that there is a Master Plan.

Here is a parable to what real *bitachon* feels like.

Chapter Twenty-Nine
What Real Bitachon Feels Like

Imagine a five-year-old, walking with her mother into the hospital for her second chemotherapy treatment. The little girl knows what's coming. She remembers the pain. She understands the nausea. She knows what it's like to brush her hair and watch clumps come out. Yet, she holds her mother's hand, and goes along, because "Mommy said I need to do this."

The child doesn't understand cancer. She certainly doesn't understand how throwing up for a week cures it. But she knows that Mommy loves her. She knows that Mommy takes care of her. And she knows that Mommy knows what's best. She fully trusts her mother.

That is the type of trust we can develop in Hashem—the almost blind trust of the child. I know that Hashem is looking out for my best interests. I know that Hashem loves me more than I love myself. And I know that Hashem knows better than I do what's for my best. So I trust Hashem. I trust that Hashem is right here, in charge of my life, orchestrating the events for my ultimate good.

So I walk through life fully confident. Not confident that things will turn out as I have planned them. Not confident that life will have a Hollywood ending. But confident that Hashem has chosen the best path for me, and is leading me down it. So I take Hashem's hand, so to speak, and walk with unwavering trust.

▶ Taking Control of My Thoughts

One of the best techniques to grow in trusting Hashem is to memorize certain phrases and repeat them over and over like a mantra: *Hashem loves me more than I love myself. Hashem knows better than I do what is for my best.*

When I say these phrases again and again, they start to sink in. I begin to recognize on an *emotional level* that "I don't really know." I learn to trust in Hashem's wisdom and kindness. And then I can do that which we humans find so difficult to do—accept what Hashem has decreed with joy.

Real *bitachon* takes a lifetime to develop. It's a growth process, with many steps along the journey. Each of the *Avos* and *Imahos* had many, many difficult life situations—not

I know that Hashem knows better than I do what's for my best. So I trust Hashem.

because Hashem couldn't do any better or because He was uncaring, but because we can't learn *bitachon* in the *beis midrash*. We can't learn to trust Hashem from a book or a tape. It's only when we are challenged by life situations that we are forced to respond. Do we transcend or do we just crumble? Do we search for the bigger picture, for the reason why Hashem might be doing this? Or are we left with questions and complaints about the way He runs the world?

▶ Where This Leaves Us

By focusing on the four levels of *emunah*, we see Hashem actively running the world. We see the Master Plan. And then by recognizing Hashem's love for us, and acknowledging His great wisdom, we learn to trust Him.

Will I know exactly why things happen? Maybe not. Will I one day know all the answers to all the questions of life? Doubtful. But it doesn't matter. There are many, many things I don't know. But just because I don't know doesn't mean Hashem doesn't know. And just because I have a question doesn't mean that Hashem doesn't have an answer. I know that Hashem loves me, and I know that He knows better than I do what's for my best. And that's enough for me.

And now we are ready. We are ready to explore the proper way to search for a spouse. What is the correct *hishtadlus*?

▶ Chapter Thirty
The Bashert Test

We have arrived. It has been a bit of a journey, but we are ready to apply the theoretical concepts of *bitachon* to the real world issue of dating. The question is: what is the correct approach when dating?

The first step is to recognize that Hashem has carefully chosen the ideal match for you, and He wants you to find him or her. But, that person might not resemble the image that you have fashioned in your mind. He may not have the qualities that you think are essential, and she may come with other traits that you don't think are particularly helpful.

And this is the critical point—the point that most people

miss, the point that causes so much misery. It's not your job to know. You can't know. That's Hashem's job.

Hashem is the wise and generous Creator. Hashem knows the future as He knows the past. Hashem knows better than you do what's best for you. And Hashem has selected the ideal match for you. Your job is to go out and find him.

To make it easier, Hashem has given us an intuition to know who that person is. That intuition is similar to the intuition that guides us in other areas of life.

▶ Choosing a Career

The Chovos HaLevovos (*Sha'ar Bitachon* 3) explains that Hashem implanted into each species of animal the tools and the aptitude to hunt for a particular food and the appetite for it. The cow desires grass. The cat craves the mouse. The robin hungers for the worm. These are natural instincts that direct the animal toward what it needs for its sustenance.

So, too, with man. In order to help us earn a living, Hashem implanted in each person an inclination toward a particular type of work. Some people like to work with their hands. Some individuals are real numbers people. Some are natural businessmen. When my son was six years old, he was already buying and selling stuff. I said to my wife, "It's pretty clear what he should be doing to earn a living."

Hashem gave each person certain skills and the preference for a specific profession in order to sup-

▶ *Hashem knows better than you do what's best for you. And Hashem has selected the ideal match for you.*

port themselves. When choosing a career, the correct *hishtadlus* is to follow that predisposition. That's what Hashem wants that person to do in order to earn a living.

So, too, when choosing a spouse. Hashem gave us the instinct to recognize our *bashert*. The system that we use to identify that person has two parts to it.

Chapter Thirty-One
The Paper Test

The first is done before the two meet. Ideally, before anyone has seen anyone and certainly before there is any involvement or emotional investment, you take the "paper test."

The paper test consists of asking the question: "On paper, do they match?" Are they looking for the same things in life? Do they share a similar outlook? Do they have compatible aspirations for their home? For their families? For life? If he intends to learn for the next ten years, and she only shops in Saks Fifth Avenue—we have a problem.

The paper test determines from an objective standpoint whether this is a good match. That doesn't mean, "Do they have the same sense of humor?" "Are they equally intelligent?" "Are they similar in personality?" Those are *compatibility* issues—issues that only *they* can answer—and only in the second stage of the process.

The paper test is also where you look for things that you won't see on the date. Is she emotionally stable? Does he have a drinking problem? Are there things in his past that might prevent him from being a supportive husband?

Assuming that the two are holding in about the same place in life, and there are no skeletons in the closet, they meet. Here, however, is where most people make their mistake.

▶ Getting It Almost Right

Mark Twain used to say the difference between *almost* the right word and the *right* word is the difference between lightning and the lightning bug—a mighty big difference. In a similar sense, the difference between the way people date and the way they *should* be dating is often worlds apart.

The reason you meet isn't because you are looking for "the best girl in Brooklyn" or for "the person with the best *middos*." Nor are you searching for "the person you want to spend your life with." You are looking for the person who was *chosen* for you.

> *The reason you meet isn't because you are looking for "the best girl in Brooklyn" or for "the person with the best middos."*

Not the one who comes closest to your image of what you want. Not someone who's tall or short, fat or skinny, smart or dumb, introverted or extroverted. You are looking for your *bashert*—and you don't know what she looks like, what her personality is like, what type of family she comes from, or even what type of person she is. There is only one way to know if she is the one—you take the *Bashert Test*.

Chapter Thirty-Two
The Bashert Test

The *Bashert Test* consists of meeting this person and seeing how you feel. Do you feel comfortable? Do you enjoy her company? Does it just sort of feel right?

Not deep, mad, passionate love. Not fireworks being shot off rooftops. Not even "Wow!" Just, does it feel natural? Your *hishtadlus* is to see if you feel an intuitive sense that this is the *right one.*

The questions to ask yourself are: Did I enjoy the dates? Do I look forward to seeing her again? Does it sort of seem to click?

There need not be any high level emotionality. No heart palpations and no shortness of breath. (Those are sure signs of infatuation, which if anything may cloud your vision.) Just an inner sense of peace. A feeling that it's natural. We enjoy being with each other. It somehow feels like I've known her all of my life.

You're looking for a feeling that this is the right one. When you have that, you move forward with the confidence that Hashem runs the world and that He has guided you to your *bashert*. And that is the point—Hashem has made the choice; you are out there to find the one that Hashem has chosen for you.

▶ She's Not What I'm Looking For

While this system may sound simple to implement—it's not. Most people have such entrenched notions of what they *need* that they won't allow themselves to just let it flow. And it seems that no matter how much they try, they keep coming back to the same obstacle.

▶ Chapter Thirty-Three

Beating the System

I got a call from a fellow who said, "*Rebbe*, you have to help me."

"Sure, sure. What's up?" I replied.

"Well, I was set up with this girl, and I think that I'm going to fall for her."

"That's great. So what's the problem?"

"What's the problem? That's the problem. She's not what I'm looking for! I want a girl who..." and he went on to list the "Miss Potato Head" qualities that he needed to be *truly* happy.

It took me almost an hour to help him see what he was doing.

He had a clear image of the kind of girl he was going to marry, and this young woman did not fit that picture. But that was the problem—he wasn't looking for his *bashert*. He was out looking for his choice—the woman that he fashioned in the image that he formed—and he was convinced that nothing but that would bring him lasting happiness. He wasn't focused on the fact that it's Hashem's job to create people. And it's Hashem's job to find matches for those people.

The proper way to go out is to forget all the criteria, skip the laundry lists, drop all the "I needs" and "I wants," and ask only one question: how do I feel about this person. Not, is she the best girl I can get? Not even, is she the best one for me? Or, do I see myself in twenty years from now being happy with her?

Ask yourself how you feel *now*. Is there a certain comfort level? Does it just seem to be right? If she passed the paper test, and the answer to this question is yes, then that is the sign that she is the right person. She is the person who was predetermined by Hashem for you. You've done your proper *hishtadlus*. Now you move forward with confidence and assurance that Hashem has predetermined the one that is right for you and brought her to you.

▶ Thirty-Two Reasons to Drop Someone

One of the complications with this system is that when a person has a feeling that this is the right one, they won't allow themselves to feel it. "I need someone smarter, or taller, or richer, or funnier, or more

> He wasn't focused on the fact that it's Hashem's job to create people. And it's Hashem's job to find matches for those people.

easygoing, or more driven," or whatever imaginable attribute that people can think up. So they say no.

Because this happens so often, I hope you'll excuse me for listing some of the more common "reasons" for saying no.

"He's not smart enough."

"He's too smart."

"He's very smart, but not the kind of smart I'm looking for."

"His family isn't good enough."

"His family is too good."

"His family is perfect, but I need a *ba'al teshuvah*."

"I don't like her looks."

"She looks too good."

"Her looks are great, but it's not the look I'm looking for."

Too tall. Too short. Too smart. Too dumb. Too worldly. Too sheltered. Too narrow. Too broad. Too plain. Too fancy. The list goes on and on.

Now you may ask, aren't these things important? Good family, smart, and attractive? Aren't they huge contributors to the success of a marriage? The answer is that they are incredibly important, and if you were putting together your Mrs. Potato Head, I think you should grab a whole big bunch of all of them. But that is the point. You aren't creating your *bashert*; you are searching for her. And you don't know whether she is smart, or pretty, or comes from a good family or not. There is only one thing that you will know about her—that she is the one that Hashem picked for you. The way you tell that is by allowing your *heart* to tell you.

▶ Doesn't Attraction Matter?

You may ask, but don't I have to think she's pretty? How can I marry a woman if I don't feel that she's attractive?

The answer is yes, you should be attracted, and if you aren't and that bothers you, it might be an indicator that she isn't the right one for you.

But it might not be, and here is where things get tricky. If you like her but don't feel attracted, or you enjoy the dates but it just seems kind of flat, this means you have a question and you should speak to someone older and wiser for advice. The fact that you aren't attracted to her may be a sign that she isn't right for you.

But only too often what happens is that she is pretty enough for you. But... she's not pretty enough for your sisters, your mother, your buddies, or your Hollywood notion of what a wife should look like.

And so you won't allow yourself to feel that attraction.

▶ The Other Side of the Fence

And this doesn't only apply to men. A woman might be going out with someone, and she'll say, "It's going well, but..." And there is something blocking her from moving forward—but she can't quite put her finger on it.

It may well be that he isn't the right person for her. However, there are many times that she is stopping herself from feeling that it's a good fit because (and now fill in the blank):

She doesn't think he will be successful; she doesn't like the family he comes from; she doesn't feel that her brothers will respect him. Or what will her friends think? Or her aunt? Or her dorm counselor? Or a whole host of other reasons that only she knows.

That is when she needs help sorting out her feelings, and she should speak to someone older and wiser for direction.

A word of caution: older means older, and wiser means wiser. Only too often I have asked a nineteen-year-old girl if she asked advice before deciding to say "no." And she said, "Absolutely. I asked my friend, and she's married, so she knows."

"I see," I would say. "And how old is this friend of yours?"

"Why, she's at least twenty."

To be candid, it's hard to believe that a twenty-year-old has the wisdom and life experience to offer much guidance in these situations. And it's prudent to find someone who has the vision and *da'as Torah* to guide you properly.

Most often, that guidance is to help you sort out what is realistic, what you should be looking for, and more than anything, what you are feeling. At the end of the day, the decision is yours. Hashem gave you an inner guidance system: the superb set of emotions, understandings, and intuitions that we call your heart. Sometimes, however, you need help sorting through exactly what you're feeling. And that's where it's invaluable to have someone older and wiser to guide you.

But the guidance isn't to make the decision for you. It's to help you focus on how you feel. Your heart may know, but cutting through the static and asking yourself, "What do I honestly feel?" isn't always that easy.

I once saw a glaring example of this.

> Chapter Thirty-Four

I Can't Commit

I was discussing a dating situation with a young man who listed the reasons he felt a certain girl was right for him. But then there was this and this and this. Repeatedly it was coming back to, "On the one hand, I think she's the right one, but, on the other, I don't."

The troubling part was that he wasn't young, and this wasn't the first time that they had gone out. They had started and stopped dating a number of times already.

At a certain point, I said to him, "What we need is Eliyahu HaNavi. If we had a prophet here, he would tell us either that she's the right one for you, but you can't commit to marriage, or you can't commit to her because she's not the one that's right for you. But that's the question. Is she the one that Hashem chose for you?"

At which point he said in a low voice, "She is the one that's right for me. But I'm angry at Hashem for it."

"Stop! Stop!" I cried. "What did you say? Say those exact words again."

"She is the one that's right for me," he said louder this time, "but I'm angry at Hashem for it."

"That's it!" I said. "You just hit it right on the head. In your heart, you know that it's right, but you feel that you won't be happy because you need something else. But that's exactly the point—you feel one way and Hashem feels the other. You feel that you need such and such qualities to have a successful marriage. And Hashem feels differently. So there is really only one question: who do you trust—you or Hashem? I think that there are some things that are just better left up to Hashem."

As comical as it sounds, that's what it boils down to. Who is picking—me or Hashem? And while this may be difficult to put into practice, the concept couldn't be simpler. The perspective is that Hashem has chosen for me the *perfect* life's partner, and Hashem wants me to find him. That person might not fit my preconceived idea of what it is I think I need, or what it is I want, but he is the one that's best for me. And that is what I'm looking for—my *bashert*.

▶ What Difference Does It Make Anyway?

At this point you might be tempted to ask, "What difference does it make if I go out the right way or the wrong way? Either way, if it's *bashert*, it's *bashert*! If Hashem meant for it to happen, it will happen. And if it doesn't happen, it wasn't meant to be. Isn't that the whole concept of *bashert*?"

Unfortunately, it's not so simple.

Chapter Thirty-Five

Bashert Doesn't Mean That It Has to Be

> *The amount of money a man is to make that year is set on Rosh Hashanah and sealed on Yom Kippur.*
>
> [*Beitzah* 16a]

Imagine it is Rosh Hashanah. I am standing in *shul* when suddenly a loud voice booms: "RABBI!"

"Yes..." I meekly respond.

"I HAVE BEEN SENT FROM HEAVEN TO DELIVER A MESSAGE."

"Yes, yes. Tell me. Please tell me. What is it?"

"THEY SENT ME TO TELL YOU THAT THIS YEAR, YOU WILL MAKE A MILLION DOLLARS."

"Oh my goodness! A million dollars! Wow! Wow! Thank you."

Now that I know my fate for the year, I say to myself, "This is great. I am guaranteed to make a fortune. All I have to do is sit back and wait for it to unfold. What could be better?"

So I take the year off. Why work? Why exert myself? I quit my day job. I don't even look at the newspapers. I know what's going to be. I lay back and wait for the money to come rolling in.

What do you think is going to happen?

Most likely, what's going to happen is that I am going to go hungry that year. Because when a decree is set on Rosh Hashanah, it doesn't mean that it has to happen. It means it is *available*, and I have to do my part to bring it about.

Many life situations are decided on Rosh Hashanah. Will I live or die? Will I enjoy health and well-being or not? Will I have success or not? Will I find my *bashert* this year? Will I have children? Each issue is weighed and measured, and then the decree is set. Hashem, in His infinite wisdom, has determined what is best for me and He has made it *accessible* to me. Now I have to do my part and act in the way of nature and go and take it.

To earn a living, I have to get a job. To remain healthy, I need to eat properly and exercise. To get married, I must go out and find my *bashert*. If I put in the effort, then Hashem will arrange that the right thing will happen—in the right way and at the right time. But if I don't put in that effort, then all bets are off. Possibly Hashem may arrange

> *When a decree is set on Rosh Hashanah, it doesn't mean that it has to happen.*

for it to happen anyway, but more likely, it won't come about. Then, what would have been best for me and what has been set for me is lost—because I didn't do my part.

The point is that Hashem doesn't handcuff a person to a given decree. I still have free will. And just because something was decreed, it doesn't mean that it has to come about. *Bashert* means it has been made available. And it's my job to go out and take what Hashem has arranged for me.

▶ Passing Up Your Bashert

A young man once asked the Steipler Gaon, *zt"l*, "When will I find my *bashert*?" The Steipler looked at the young man and replied, "You already passed her up when you were looking for the perfect girl."

You can pass up your *bashert*. Hashem prepares the right person and arranges that the two of you should meet, but you still have free will. If you wake up one day and say, "Forget this whole dating thing. I'm just not getting married," most likely you won't. The fact that Hashem prepared someone for you doesn't force you to accept her. And you can pass her by for any number of reasons.

And now we come to what may well be one of the tragedies of modern times.

▶ Chapter Thirty-Six

I Can't Find My Bashert

It seems that we are seeing more and more older singles than ever before. Good people. *Frum* people. Smart. Talented. Put together. And they look and look, yet they can't find the right one. They've gone out with this one and with that one. They went to this *shadchan* and to that one. This singles event and that weekend. All to no avail. They're not getting any younger—yet they just can't find the one.

And they raise their voice in an honest plea, "What does Hashem want from me? All I want to do is settle down and raise a Jewish family. Hashem, why won't You help me?"

▶ Why?

The question is: why? Why is it that we are seeing more and more of this today? While there may not be a one-size-fits-all answer to this question, there is a perspective that is worth contemplating.

There are times when a person does everything he should, and for various reasons, Hashem sees that this isn't the right time. But often, that's not the case. If you speak to older singles about their dating experiences, often the reason they can't find their *bashert* is obvious: they dumped him. For this reason or for that. Too much this or too much that. Not enough this or not enough that. The one thing they all have in common is, "He's just not for me. He's a good guy. He has a lot of positive qualities. But he's not what I'm looking for." And they go back to the trail, searching, ever searching, for their Mr. Potato Head. And they find themselves ten years older and not much wiser, still looking for him.

While this isn't always the case, unfortunately it isn't that rare either. So at the risk of raising the ire of some innocent people, I would like to address "the big complaint."

Chapter Thirty-Seven

So You Want Me to Settle?

"So what you're saying is that I shouldn't be picky. I should just accept any old thing that walks in the door. As long as he can chew his food, and tie his own laces, I should marry him. You want me to settle!"

The answer to this is—yes! One hundred percent. You should settle. You should settle for that which Hashem has destined for you. You should stop playing God. You should stop pretending to know what you need to be happy. You should accept the fact that Hashem has chosen the right person for you. You should trust Him. And there is a tremendous amount of suffering that needn't be—if people would just do what they should.

▶ I'm Just Not Sure

Nevertheless, that is all well and good in theory, but what happens if you sort of, kind of, feel this person is the right one—but you're just not sure? What do you do?

So, again, the first thing you do is speak the situation over with someone older and wiser than you, the main goal being to help you sort out your feelings and help you identify exactly what you feel.

It's also the time to ask Hashem for help. (It's always the time to ask Hashem for help, but especially now.) You turn to Hashem and say: "Hashem, I want to serve You. I want to find the one that You have arranged for me. Please guide me."

▶ But I'm Just Not Sure

But what happens if you did all this and you still don't know? You took the paper test—he passed with flying colors. You did the *bashert* test—it went smooth as glass. You still weren't certain, so you *davened* and *davened*. Then you went to someone older and wiser. And now it's clear. You know it—he's the right one, but... you still can't commit.

Sometimes the answer is you just have to jump. But there are times when something else is playing in the background.

► Chapter Thirty-Eight

But I'm Not Madly, Passionately in Love

Sometimes people who are close to getting engaged experience fear. As in, "I'm not crazy about her. I mean, I like her and everything, but I don't feel infatuation now. So how can I be certain that she is the right one, and how can I know that I will ever love her?"

This fear is based on the assumption that the love in marriage comes from infatuation that solidifies into something deeper, as if the bond of love is made up of infatuation that sort of grows up.

That isn't the way it works. Infatuation is a temporary state that ends. It was created to start things off, and then it fades away and is gone—never to be heard from again.

Ask a happily married, older couple if the feelings they have toward one another now have anything to do with what they felt when they were "young and in love." The answer is almost always no. Because true love isn't infatuation grown up. It is a fundamentally different set of feelings and emotions. It's a bond based on commitment, devotion, and dedication. It may have been helped along by a sense of infatuation and desire, but that is just one of the many catalysts that helps to form a real attachment.

Some couples start with more infatuation; some start with less. But it isn't relevant—because the feelings are illusory. It's like a drug-induced state. Some drugs cause one sensation; some cause another. Some drugs are more powerful; some are less—but they all wear off. Hashem created the sense of infatuation to help things move along in the beginning. But just as it isn't a criterion for choosing a spouse, it isn't a vital ingredient in a successful marriage. Many great marriages have begun with minimal initial excitement and wow. And most marriages that begin with fireworks and explosions of passion end in divorce. (Witness the over fifty-percent divorce rate in the United States.)

▶ My Friend Was One Hundred Percent Certain

You hear people say, "When my friend got engaged, he was head over heels. He was a thousand percent sure that she was the right one for him. I don't feel that, so how can I commit?"

The answer is that your friend wasn't a hundred percent sure—he was a hundred percent blind. He thought he knew. He thought he understood who she was and what he was getting into... but he didn't. Anyone who really thinks he knows is fooling himself. There is no way to know.

But more than that, it's not your job to know. Your job is to see if it feels right. That's your *hishtadlus* in this situation. If it feels like she's the right one, you have to take that leap. Not a leap of faith, not a hope against hope that there's a net below. You have to trust that Hashem brought you into this world, has watched over you since birth, and is now directing you to the right one. You close your eyes and you leap, knowing that Hashem is with you, guiding and directing you.

Now we come to a major crossroads. What happens if you find yourself deep in the dating game and realize that maybe I passed him by? Maybe it's me who passed by my *bashert*.

▶ Chapter Thirty-Nine

Maybe I Missed My Bashert

The first step is to realize that there are second chances. We've all heard our share of dating stories where the couple went out and decided it wasn't a match. They each went their separate ways, dated other people, and finally six years later, they went out again and got married.

But that's not always the case. Sometimes there is a bigger perspective involved.

▶ The Rest of the Story

I was at a *shivah* house, and an intriguing story emerged. The man who had passed away grew up in Iran and didn't get married until he was forty-five. Not that he wasn't looking—he just couldn't find the right one. Finally, after many years, he married his wife, the woman sitting *shivah*. When he died, he was ninety-three, and they had been married for forty-eight years. The interesting part was that she was only seventy-two; there had been a twenty-one year difference in age between them. And then I got to hear the "rest of the story."

The *niftar* (deceased) had been a successful businessman, and in the course of his life owned close to fifty businesses. Not every one of them did well, but over time he succeeded and prospered. Eventually, his children joined him in business, and he remained active late into his life. When he was eighty-eight years old, he was still going to work every day. At around ninety, he slowed down and would only go in three days a week. Until almost the end, he kept a hand in the business.

As I started thinking about his life, the pieces came together.

Imagine this man as a young person living in Iran, when he turns to Hashem and asks for help: "Hashem, please help me find the right one."

Nothing happens.

When he's in his late twenties, he's still praying: "Hashem, it's very difficult. Why won't You help me?"

Still, nothing.

Then he's in his thirties. "Hashem, please! I am trying to do your will. Why can't I find the right one?"

Nothing.

He's already forty. "Hashem, if not now—when?"

> *She was only seventy-two; there had been a twenty-one year difference in age between them.*

Finally, at forty-five he finds her. For the life of him, he can't figure out what took so long, but he's thankful that at last he's married.

▶ What Took So Long?

Of course, we will never know the real reason, but let's imagine that when this man first started praying, we were in Heaven and got to hear Hashem's response.

"*Yingele*, you don't understand. You have a long life ahead of you. If I match you up with a woman your age, what's going to happen? When she's in her sixties, she'll be slowing down. But not you—you'll still be going strong. When she hits seventy, she's going to want to rest and take it easy. But you'll be active, moving, doing. Then shortly after that, she'll need a walker, then a nursing home, and before you know it, she'll be gone. And then you'll be alone—with many more years to go. It's so hard to be alone when you're old. You're young now—you have friends, things to keep you busy. I know it's hard to wait, but please be patient. The one that's right for you is still in diapers!"

Naturally, we mortals aren't privy to conversations held Above, but sometimes, many years after the events, we are able to see the big picture and we see how Hashem was carefully orchestrating our lives.

The point though is that we don't know. We don't know what we need, we don't know how things will turn out, and we don't know what is for our best. But we can have *bitachon*.

Bitachon is knowing that Hashem is looking out for my best interests. It is recognizing that Hashem knows better than I do what is for my best. In certain areas it's difficult to see this—I feel

I know better. But some things are clearly better left to Hashem. And finding one's spouse is in this category.

When I come to this recognition, I can then turn to Hashem and say, "Master of the Universe, you have chosen the one that's right, the one who's perfect for me. I understand that I have to do my part, that I have to go and look. But please guide me, not to the one I think I need, not to the one that I think I want, but to the one that You know is best for me—my *bashert*."

While we could end this book here, there is still one more point that is essential.

Chapter Forty

Keeping Your Bashert

We live in an age where the very social fabric of society seems to be tearing apart at the seams. Divorce rates in the western world hover at fifty percent. And that's only for first marriages. Second marriages have an even higher failure rate. And third marriages a higher failure rate still. One study done by the University of Washington showed that based on census data, the divorce rate for recent marriages was actually sixty-seven percent. Besides the personal misery, the biggest cost is that the concept of raising children in a stable home seems to be a relic of the past.

Divorce rates in the western world hover at fifty percent. And that's only for first marriages.

And while it's true that we Jews are a nation separate and above the rest of the world, it affects us as well. Divorce in our community has also risen to an alarming rate.

While there are many factors that affect the divorce rate, and this isn't a book of techniques for improving your marriage, there is one perspective that is vital for the success of your marriage.

▶ A Bit of Wisdom

A number of years ago, I brought a couple to my *rebbe*, the *rosh ha-yeshiva*, *zt"l*. They hadn't been married very long, and the fights were regular and nasty. Things didn't look too promising.

The *rosh ha-yeshiva* took the time to speak to them for a while. And from that point on, their marriage took a turn for the better and continued to improve. They are happily married for many years now.

You might be wondering what "magical words" the *rosh ha-yeshiva* said. Was it Kabbalah? Or at least ruach ha-kodesh?

It was neither. It was the *rosh ha-yeshiva's* wisdom that saved their marriage. He brought them both into his office and listened carefully to what each one had to say. He then asked the young man to step outside, and he turned to the woman and asked her what was going on. The *rosh ha-yeshiva* listened very carefully as she spoke and he picked up a sense of what the problem was. The husband felt that his new wife wasn't up to his level. It seems that this man was quite successful in *yeshiva*, and he held of himself— maybe a tad too much.

The *rosh ha-yeshiva* then called the husband into his office, and his first remark was, "She's a very *chashuvah* girl. I'm very impressed with her." The *rosh ha-yeshiva* went on to ask another question or two, and then repeated, "She's a very *chashuvah* girl. I'm very impressed." He then followed with a few more questions and some comments, and then a third time the *rosh ha-yeshiva* repeated, "She's a very *chashuvah* girl. I'm very impressed."

This conversation changed their marriage. How? Because this young man looked up to the *rosh ha-yeshiva* as a Torah sage. Here was a *gadol b' Yisrael* giving his wife the stamp of approval. "Obviously, there's a lot more to her than I realized," he thought. And that transformed their marriage.

▶ Who Made This Shidduch?

The thought that you should keep in the forefront of your mind is that the Creator of the heavens and the earth handpicked your spouse to be your partner in life. And most likely, Hashem knows what He's doing. Most likely, Hashem got it right.

If you are wondering why this concept is so critical for the success of a marriage, it shouldn't be that much of a mystery.

▶ Chapter Forty-One
I Made the Biggest Mistake of My Life

At some point in most marriages, either the husband, or the wife, or both realize that things aren't going as they should be. And the process starts:

"This isn't what I expected in marriage," he mutters to himself.

"I never bargained for this," she thinks.

"To be quite frank," he confides to his friend, "I'm not sure how much I like her, let alone love her."

And this continues on and off for a while until that crashing realization hits him, and he screams out: "I made the biggest mistake of my life. I married the wrong person!"

It's at that very moment that he has to ask himself a critical question, a question that frames every other assumption and attitude that he has about marriage.

That question is: who made this match? Who brought us together?

Asked in this way, the question is the answer. Because once he understands that Hashem brought this person to him, and him to this person, he is ready for the very first rule in a successful marriage.

Chapter Forty-Two
It's About Growth

A successful marriage is about two people joining together in peace, harmony, and love. For that to happen, both parties have to be giving, caring, generous people who have the maturity to put aside their own self-interests and self-gratification and devote themselves to another person's needs. Most of us aren't ready for that for a long, long time.

And that's the first rule about marriage. A solid, happy marriage demands that both partners change. It requires significant growth. And there's a lot of learning on the job.

But it's not by accident that marriage requires change and demands work. Hashem created us with all the tools, motivations, and situations that we need to reach our level of spiritual perfection. While a perfect marriage is partially about finding a helpmate, it's also a stage setting that demands growth.

On the most basic level, it's about learning to put another human being's needs before your own. When a baby is born, that baby is one hundred percent selfish. When the baby is hungry, the baby cries. When the baby is wet, the baby cries. When the baby is cranky, the baby cries. An infant only knows its own needs and isn't equipped to care about another person. As we mature, we are supposed to become caring and sensitive to others. But this doesn't come naturally—it requires a lot of work and a lot of focus. For most of us (men especially), marriage is the first time that we actually have to put someone else's needs before our own. It's the first time that we leave that sheltered cocoon of "my needs," "my wants," and "my desires," and look out for the interest of another. For the first time in our lives, we begin to act like Hashem—focused on giving, caring, and nurturing someone else. So, in that sense, marriage as an institution is a huge growth opportunity.

▶ On a Personal Level

But on a personal level, it is equally significant. Each of us has areas that we need to work on. For one person, it might be learning to be patient. For another, it might be working on his temper. For yet another, it might be about becoming less arrogant. Everyone has a particular weakness that requires improvement.

Hashem handcrafts the perfect situation for each person's growth. Challenging, yet doable. Demanding, yet within reach. When Hashem brings together a couple, it is for the purpose of the two joining and making a strong whole, and for the two to help complete one another. Included in that is perfecting the area that each of them needs to improve.

One of the things we humans find difficult is change. And while we are very skilled at seeing the areas that other people need to develop, turning that same critical eye to ourselves is something we rarely do.

And so, what often happens in a marriage is that each partner sees only too well what the other one is doing wrong—but they do not see their part in the picture.

I once got a chance to see a glaring example of this.

▶ Chapter Forty-Three

One Side of
the Story

One day, I received a phone call from a young man. He was crying, when he said to me, "*Rebbe*, she left me. She just left. Without a reason! If she would be willing to work on it, to go for counseling, it would be one thing. But she just walked out. And she won't even discuss it."

I had a hard time responding. I had been working with this couple for two years, taking them from marriage counselor to marriage counselor, and I couldn't get the guy to stop screaming, ranting, and yelling at his wife. He was the most abusive husband I had ever dealt with. The words he would scream at his wife would make your hair stand on end.

"She just left. Without a reason..." Mmmmmmmm....

What was going on was quite simple. He had a temper. He would say things in anger, and ten minutes later, he would calm down and apologize for what he had said, explaining that he hadn't really meant it. She, on the other hand, was the recipient of those barbs. The person she considered her closest friend and confidant would turn around time and again and viciously cut into her. It wasn't so easy for her to forget. By the next day, he didn't even remember that he had said hurtful words, and he was ready to start fresh. But she still harbored the wounds of his stabs, and she wasn't able to just move on. This cycle continued and continued until she could no longer bear it.

▶ It Applies to Me

While this example is extreme, the concept is universal. When it's me that gets hurt, I find it hard to forget. But when it's someone else that I hurt, I find it hard to remember. My own pain—I am acutely sensitive to. The pain I cause to others—I barely notice.

That is human nature. And it is one of the great challenges of growth and one of the great challenges of marriage. I have to love my spouse, care for my spouse, and stop doing those things that annoy her. I have to change. And change doesn't come easy. It's much easier to put the blame somewhere else. It's much easier to point a finger at another party. And for me to have the emotional bandwidth to work on my things, I have to know that things can change.

And so, one of the tools to make a marriage work is to say over and over and over again: "Who made this match? Who brought this about? It's Hashem's world, and He put us together."

When a person approaches marriage with the right attitude,

it can be the most fulfilling, beautiful experience imaginable. But you have to be ready for it. You have to be ready to grow. You have to be ready to accept that your image of the perfect spouse may not be what Hashem knows is for your best. And you have to be ready to change.

There is, however, one more perspective that is critical for relating to this issue and even more critical for relating to life.

Chapter Forty-Four

I Never Promised You a Rose Garden

> *"And they sat to eat bread, and they lifted their eyes and saw a caravan of Yishma'elim coming from Gilad, and their camels were carrying spices, balsam, and birthwort to bring down to Egypt."*
>
> [*Bereishis* 37:25]

▶ The Most Difficult Period in Yosef's Life

Yosef was about to begin the most difficult period of his life. His own brothers had left him to die in a pit of scorpions. He would soon be sold numerous times as a slave, and then he would spend twelve months being hounded by the wife of his master, followed by imprisonment in a dank, dark dungeon where he would not see the light of day for twelve years. Clearly, Yosef was heading for hard times.

Rashi tells us that this *pasuk* shows us the great reward that is given to *tzaddikim*. When Yosef was bound and sold as a slave, the wagon that took him down to Egypt was carrying spices that emitted a fragrant smell. Normally, the Arab caravans carried kerosene that gives off an obnoxious odor. Clearly, Hashem loved Yosef and arranged for something out of the ordinary to make the journey more pleasant for him.

The obvious question on this Rashi is that if the Torah wants to show us the reward for *tzaddikim*, it would have done a much more convincing job by saving Yosef from this entire ordeal. If Hashem is watching over *tzaddikim* and giving them great reward, then why couldn't He just save Yosef from all of the suffering that he was about to endure?

▶ A Comfortable Pillow in the Ambulance

This is comparable to a situation in which a man is in a near fatal car crash that breaks almost every bone in his body. The Hatzalah crew rushes to the scene, puts him on a stretcher, and as they are speeding to the hospital, his friend riding with him says, "Look how Hashem watches over you. You even have a comfortable pillow under your head." That man would have the right to ask, "If Hashem is concerned with my well-being, why didn't He arrange for the drunk driver who hit me to crash into a pole instead of my car? Save me from the accident; don't give my broken neck a comfortable pillow to lie on!"

▶ Some Life Situations Are Inevitable

The answer to this question seems to be that there are certain situations in life that are unavoidable—not because Hashem isn't capable of preventing them, but quite the opposite—because Hashem orchestrated them according to the needs of that person or that generation.

Yosef was to be sold as a slave, and in that state brought down to Mitzrayim. As the prelude to his future, the future of his family, and the future of the Jewish nation, this was a vital ingredient. Ultimately, for his destiny and for the good of the Jewish nation, this situation needed to happen. It was part of the Master Plan.

However, even within the difficult times, Hashem showed loving-kindness to Yosef. He had to be sold as a slave, but why should he suffer unnecessarily? The Arabs normally carried petroleum; why should Yosef have to suffer the offensive odor? For that reason, Hashem arranged something very uncharacteristic—the caravan was carrying fragrant spices and not oil.

▶ All Suffering Is Carefully Weighed and Measured

There is a great lesson for us to take from this. In life, we will suffer through many situations, trials, and tribulations. Not only are they are part of life, they are needed for our growth so that we can reach the purpose for which we were put on this planet. In that sense, they are inevitable. Not because Hashem is uncaring, but because we need them. They are for our good. In the scheme of life, they serve us well, but along with them comes some suffering. The amount of suffering that a person experiences on this planet is weighed, measured, and administered in exact dosages.

The pain is delivered precisely and exactly, not an iota more and not an iota less. We get exactly the measure we need.

Many times, it is clear that Hashem is bringing pain, pre-planned and preordained, right to my doorstep. But it is hard to see why it is for my good and that Hashem is doing it out of loving-kindness.

▶ Seeing the Kindness in the Torture

When I discover the kindness within the torture, when I find the "comfortable pillow in the ambulance," this changes my perspective of the entire situation. It reminds me that Hashem cares for me and has brought about this event for my good. I may not see how it is good, I may not yet understand how it is for my best, but I recognize that Hashem orchestrates it. I see that Hashem has gone out of His way, so to speak, to make at least part of my situation more comfortable. This shows me the great love that Hashem has for me. It allows me to know that just as the pillow was put there out of love, so, too, were the rest of the circumstances. This colors the entire situation in a different light, allowing me to understand that it was brought by Hashem, and despite the pain and suffering, it is something that I need for my good.

This is a perspective that is needed in order to relate to Hashem's Divine plan and is vital for our success in life. And that brings us to a final point.

▶ Chapter Forty-Five

The Journey's End

Hashem is loving, kind, and generous. Hashem created us to share of His good. Hashem put us into this world to give us the opportunity to reach our level of perfection so that we can enjoy great reward for eternity.

To do that, Hashem placed us into the ideal life setting for each individual. Riches or poverty, health or sickness, success or failure—these are but roles that we play on the stage of life. Who we are at the end of the journey is who we have made ourselves into, and who we will be forever.

While the journey is fleeting and not significant in itself, Hashem wants us to enjoy even this brief part of life. And so

Hashem created many features and put them into this corridor for our enjoyment. Tastes, aromas, flavors, and sights—so many features that serve no functional purpose other than for us to benefit from during our time here.

To aid us and to make the journey more pleasant, Hashem provides each of us with a life's partner. That match is the perfect soul mate for me, the one created and suited to be my companion, my partner, and my friend. Together we are able to create a life of harmony and bliss, each one helping and supporting the other. It is a partnership of the deepest levels. It begins in this world and continues on into the next. We are eternally bound—together, forever.

Because of the complexity of the human and the uniqueness of each person's life, only our Creator with His infinite wisdom can choose the perfect match for us. However, Hashem created this world with free will. So at no time is man handcuffed to a particular fate, and Hashem won't force someone to choose—even if it's for his good. Nevertheless, Hashem only wishes for our best and Hashem waits for our success. So, we turn to Him for direction and we rely on Him to guide us.

A successful marriage is the most nourishing relationship possible. Both partners join as one to form a whole in harmony, joy, peace, and security. More than just an aid to the journey, however, marriage itself is one of the stage settings of life that helps a person reach his level of perfection.

The human is made up of two distinct parts: half angel from up high, and half animal from below. Man is in perfect balance, capable of choosing his path and able to create his destiny. When man exercises his higher soul, he perfects himself and all of creation along with him. When he gives into his base desires, he becomes lower than those animals that were created to serve him.

Only Hashem is perfect. Our measure of perfection is how much like Hashem we are. When two mortals join together in marriage, they are challenged to transcend their physical limitations. They are called upon to put another's concerns before their own. The self-serving creature is called upon to act in the role of the giver—generous and magnanimous, loving and kindly. Together, they are called to live in an elevated existence. They are challenged to be like Hashem, as much as a human is able.

For some, finding their mate is quick and painless; for others, it takes a while. For everyone, there are ups and downs and plenty of bumps along the road. That's not a sign that the marriage isn't working. Quite the opposite, it's often an indicator that each partner is being challenged to change, to grow.

In the end, a successful marriage is the most tender, meaningful relationship that can be: the joining together of two souls on the highest plane where each partner loses their self-centered nature and joins a harmonious, loving relationship. They cease being two individuals apart and become two parts to one whole.

While the passage takes work, the path is pleasant and the rewards are great.

May your journey be successful; may your path be sweet.

Ben Tzion Shafier
25 Kislev, Chanukah 5772

▶ Afterthoughts

▶ All Suffering Is Carefully Weighed and Measured

Writing on a topic as weighty and lofty as *emunah* and *bitachon* borders on the audacious. Even as I strove to cling to the path that the *Chovos HaLevovos* laid out for us, there is an inherent danger in interpreting and applying a fundamental work that was written almost a thousand years ago. The times were different, the people were different, and there is much room for error. For that reason, I am especially appreciative of those who read through this work and made many valuable contributions to it.

While my primary *rebbe* is the *rosh ha-yeshivah*, HaRav Alter

Henoch Lebovitz, *zt'l*, I also spent many years learning under Rabbi Davidowitz, Rosh Yeshiva of the Rochester Yeshiva, and much of my *mahalach hamchshava* was developed under his direct guidance. So I am especially appreciative of his reading through this work and making many valuable comments.

I would like to thank R' Tzvi Berkowitz, Rosh Yeshiva of Ner Israel for his thorough and insightful comments, and Rabbi Yisrael Rakowsky, Rosh Yeshiva of Ohr Somayach, Monsey for his valuable insights into the *yesodos* of *emunah*. I thank Rabbi Boruch Davidowitz, Menahel of the Rochester Yeshiva, for his help and guidance. Thanks to Rabbi Yossie Singer, Menahel of Chofetz Chaim Mesivta in Queens, and Rabbi Eli Gelb of Monsey for their assistance. I would also like thank Rebbitzen Sarah Davidowitz for her many valuable critiques and observations.

Part of this work deals with issues of science and medicine. In that area, I am deeply appreciative of the help of Dr. Robert Berman and Dr. Alexander Kushnir who have both made themselves readily available to me.

Finally as in everything I do, my most sincere appreciation goes to my life's partner, my wife. My Torah and your Torah is her Torah. May Hashem grant us many more productive and happy years together.

Where Do We Go From Here?

I hope that you have found this book meaningful. While it offers information, its primary purpose is to impart a perspective – a perspective that should be the underpinnings of everything that we do. If this book brought you to think about the big issues of life, then I consider it a success — it has done its job. The question is: where do we go from here? How do you maintain that perspective? How do you apply it to your life? What is the next step?

Certainly, there is no one answer, as this is one of the great challenges of life. To deal with this issue, a wealth of material has been developed by Torah giants over hundreds of years. The difficult part is accessing that material. Many people find applying the Mussar works a daunting task, one that just doesn't seem to work for them.

A tool that I would like to suggest is "The Shmuz." The Shmuz is exactly what the title implies, a mussar "talk" that deals with a wide range of subjects: davening, emunah, bitachon, marriage, parenting, people skills, working on anger, jealousy and humility.... At this point, there are over two hundred lectures, and the list is growing. Similar in style to the book that you have just read, the Shmuz takes the Torah sources and applies it to life – to your life in the twenty-first century.

The lectures are available in a number of portals, and one is the Shmuz.com. There you can listen, watch, read, download or podcast. I welcome you to look around the site. You will also find many other shiurim and materials there.

If you are from an earlier age, or if you try to avoid internet usage, there are still a number of ways to access the Shmuz. We have CDs of the audio, books on various topics, and you can listen to the Shmuz on Kol Halashon.

If you would like more information or would like to bring the Shmuz to your community, please call the Shmuz office at 1- 866-613-TORAH (8672). I also welcome any thoughts or comments. You can reach me by e-mail me at rebbe@theshmuz.com.

May this be a zechus for myself and those I daven for to find our basherts!

Leah Weingarten

May Hashem answer the tefilos of all those in our Shul who are searching for their special zivug.

Rabbi Chaim and Gitty Bausk
Young Israel of East Northport

לזכר נשמת

הרב שמעון בן צבי הירש
מרים עלא בת ר׳ ישראל אליעזר הכהן
פאליק בן הערצקא

Devorah and Louis
Greenspan

Dr. Ephraim P. Bartfeld   Dr. Jacqueline O. Lustig

Town and Country Pediatrics and
Family Medicine, PC

380 Main Street   Tel: (860) 274-8891
Watertown, CT 06795   Fax:(860) 274-8895

לעילוי נשמת

מרדכי בן מנחם
חנה בת יעקב אייזיק

_____

LISTING OF SHMUZIN AVAILABLE AT THESHMUZ.COM

Shmuz #1
Eternal
People

Shmuz #2
Yomim
Noraim –
Issues of
the Day

Shmuz #3
Yom Kippur –
The power of
Teshuvah

Shmuz #4
Appreciating
Olam Hazeh

Shmuz #5
Appreciating
our Wealth

Shmuz #6
Its not
Geneivah, it's
Shtick

Shmuz #7
Noach:
Understanding
Belief

Shmuz #8
Power of
Prayer

Shmuz #9
Akaidas
Yitzchak

Shmuz #10
Questioning
G-d: Finding
and keeping
your Bashert

Shmuz #11
Kibud Av of
Eisav –
Appreciating
Parents

Shmuz #12
People of
Principle

Shmuz #13
Free Will – Part
1: Nefesh Haba-
hami, Nefesh
Hasichli

Shmuz #14
Living like a
Rock

Shmuz #15
Chanukah
G-d fights Our
Wars

Shmuz #16
Olam Habba:
The Greatest
Motivator

Shmuz #17
Acquiring Olam
Habba The Easy
Way – "Every-
one needs a
Mike"

Shmuz #18
Difference Be-
tween Emunah
& BitAchon
– 4 Levels To
Emunah

Shmuz #19
Free will - Part
2: I Never
Do Anything
Wrong

Shmuz #20
Davening
- Making it
Real

Shmuz #21
Choosing a
Career

Shmuz #22
Evolution -
Does it Make
Sense?

Shmuz #23
I'll never die.
Not me. No
way.

Shmuz #24
Understand-
ing Life
Settings

Shmuz #25
They don't
make anti
Semites like
they used to

Shmuz #26
Loshon Horah
– Squander-
ing our Olam
Habbah

Shmuz #27
Respecting
the Institu-
tion – America
the Beautiful

Shmuz
#28 People
Believe what
they want to
Believe

Shmuz #29
The Busy
Generation

Shmuz #30
Anger Man-
agement

Shmuz #31
The Voice
Inside

Shmuz #32
Understanding
Nature – Put-
ting the "WOW"
back into
Nature

Shmuz #33
Where Was
G-D During
the Holo-
caust?

Shmuz #34
Israel: Ex-
alted Nation
/ Oppressed
People

Shmuz #35
Hashem and
Man: Master
and Servant
(Understanding
Humility)

Shmuz #36
For the Love
of Money

Shmuz #37
Three Types of
Miracles – The
Fifth Level of
Emunah

Shmuz #38
Where is
Hashem – The
Sixth Level of
Emunah

Shmuz #39
I Need, Needs

Shmuz #40
Acher – The
Importance
of Torah –
Founding an
Organization

Shmuz #41
Rebbe Akiva
and Rochel –
Potential of
the individual

Shmuz #42
Tricks of the
Soton

Shmuz #43
Soton out of
the Box

Shmuz #44
Bar Kamtza -
Do you
really have
Free Will?

Shmuz #45
WYSIWYG-
Developing
Willpower

Shmuz #46
Greatness of
Man- Beyond
our under-
standing

Shmuz #47
Cognitive
Restructuring

Shmuz #48
Being a Nice
Guy

Shmuz #49
Yom Kippur-
The Capacity
of a human

Shmuz #50
Bitachon
– Learning
to Trust
HASHEM

Shmuz #51
Bitachon part
II- Bitachon
& Hishtadlus
– Finding the
balance

Shmuz #52
Bitachon
Part III- The
Maaser
Shmuz

Shmuz #53
I Hate
Criticism

Shmuz #54
Understand-
ing Laziness

Shmuz #55
Staying Pure
in an
Impure World

Shmuz #56
Chanukah –
The Death
of Right and
Wrong

Shmuz #57
Torah –
Creating
Worlds

Shmuz #58
Arrogance –
Misdirected
"Greatness of
Man"

Shmuz #59
Humility –
An Issue of
Perspective

Shmuz #60
Tidal Waves
and Middas
HaDin

Shmuz #61
Heroes!

Shmuz #62
Plan Your
Life, Live
Your Plan

Shmuz #63
Davening
– Close En-
counters with
our Creator

Shmuz #64
Davening Part
II- The Love
of a Father To
A Son

Shmuz #65
Davening Part
III- The Third
System – The
Power of the
Words

Shmuz #66
Torah – The
Mark of the
Man

Shmuz #67
Understand-
ing and
Eliminating
Jealousy

Shmuz #68
People Skills

Shmuz #69
Yitzias Mitz-
raim – A War
of Ideology

Shmuz #70
Onah – The
Torah's
Sensitivity to
another's pain

Shmuz #71
Chesed:
Being Like
HASHEM

Shmuz #72
Respect : The
Students of
Rebbe Akiva

LISTING OF SHMUZIN AVAILABLE AT THESHMUZ.COM

Shmuz #73
Self Respect;
The Basis of
it All

Shmuz #74
Divaykus in
Our Times

Shmuz #75
Respect :
The Students
of Rebbe
Akiva-The Art of
Appreciation

Shmuz #76
Asking Advice

Shmuz #77
Man-Based
Morality

Shmuz #78
Kiddush
HASHEM

Shmuz #79
Reward &
Punishment

Shmuz #80
It's Never
Too Late

Shmuz #81
All for my
People

Shmuz #82
Why Me?
Understand-
ing Suffering

Shmuz #83
The Moon was
Jealous- Under-
standing the
Forces of Nature

Shmuz #84
Why Me?

Shmuz #85
MOTIVATION!

Shmuz #86
To Tell the
Truth

Shmuz #87
Self Control!

Shmuz #88
Chanukah
- The Effect
of Outside
Influences

Shmuz #89
Malbin Pnei
Chavero

Shmuz #90
Torah
L'Shmah

Shmuz #91
I Never
Forget

Shmuz #92
TACT

Shmuz #93
Shabbos-
Foundation of
our Emunah

Shmuz #94
On Being
Judgmental

Shmuz #95
Time Man-
agement

Shmuz #96
Purim III-
Sieze the
Moment

Shmuz #97
Living the
Good life

Shmuz #98
The Power
of Positive
Thinking

Shmuz #99
Men are from
Mars

Shmuz #100
Keeping The
Dream Alive

Shmuz #101
Why Pray?

Shmuz #102
Learning
To Love
HASHEM

Shmuz #103
Torah Study
- The Key To
It All

Shmuz #104
Parenting 101

Shmuz #105
Understand-
ing Life
Settings
PART II

Shmuz #106
The Power of
a Tzibbur

Shmuz #107
CHAZAK!

Shmuz #108
Servant of
HASHEM

Machlokes

Shmuz #109
Machlokes -
The Damage
of Conflict

Shmuz #110
Becoming a
Great
Individual

Shmuz #111
Sustaining
Spiritual
Growth

Shmuz #112
Chessed - The
Essence of
Judaism

Shmuz #113
Tshuvah - Two
Elements to
a Sin

Shmuz #114
Creating a
Balanced Self
Esteem

Shmuz #115
Preparing For
Yom Kipper

Shmuz #116
GROWTH

Shmuz #117
Optimism

Shmuz #118
Da'as Torah

Shmuz #119
Bris Milah

Shmuz #120
Thrift

Shmuz #121
EMES The
Whole Truth

Shmuz #122
Parenting 102

Shmuz #123
Chanukah:
Whose Side
Are You On?

Shmuz #124
Life is Like a
Box of
Chocolates

Shmuz #125
Business
Ethics

Shmuz #126
Dignity of
Man

Shmuz #127
Breaking The
Forces Of
Habits

Shmuz #128
Kiruv: The
Message &
The Medium

Shmuz #129
HaKaras
HaTov:
Recognizing
the Good

Shmuz #130
Living With
Bitachon

Shmuz #131
Working For
A Living

Shmuz #132
PURIM:
Being Human

Shmuz #133
ReJEWvinate

Shmuz #134
PARENTING
103: Setting
Limits

Shmuz #135
Imagination:
The Devil's
Playground

Shmuz #136
I'm Never
Wrong

Shmuz #137
Being
Sensitive

Shmuz #138
The Potential
& The
Present

Shmuz #139
The Power of
Speech

Shmuz #140
The Arabs
and The Jews

Shmuz #141
Parenting
Part IV: Sib-
ling Rivalry

Shmuz #142
The Power of
Laughter

Shmuz #143
Stages of
Change – Part
1: Denial

Shmuz #144
Stages of
Change Part
II: Support
Groups

Shmuz #145
Stages of
Change Part
III: Taking
Action

Shmuz #146 -
The Impact of
One Mitzvah

Shmuz #147 -
Finding G-d

Shmuz #148
Rich, Richer,
Richest - How
to be Wealthy

Shmuz #149
The System
of Teshuvah

Shmuz #150
Being a
Religious
Atheist

Shmuz #151
Be Brave,
Be Bold

Shmuz #152
In G-d's
Image

Shmuz #153
Marriage:
A Work in
Progress

Shmuz #154
Marriage: A
Work in Prog-
ress PART II

Shmuz #155
Chanukah
- Flexi-dox
Judaism

Shmuz #156
Get Out of
Debt

Shmuz #157
Learning to
Love Learn-
ing

Shmuz #158
Me & My Big
Mouth

Shmuz #159
212 Degrees
- Just One De-
gree Hotter

Shmuz #160
Purim:
Sheep to the
Slaughter and
Concert Bans

Shmuz #161
April 15th:
The Test of
Emunah

Shmuz #162
Learning to
Care

Shmuz #163
Only the
Good Die
Young

Shmuz #164
I Hate
Criticism

Shmuz #165
The Art Of
Listening

Shmuz #166
Everybody is
doing it

Shmuz #167
Sefiras Ha'Omer
Countdown
to Ka'balas
Ha'Torah

Shmuz #168
Emunah

Shmuz #169
Anger Taming
the Monster
Within

Shmuz #170
Sweet
Revenge

Shmuz #171
Don't Sweat
the Small
Stuff

Shmuz #172
The Tisha
B'Av Shmuz

Shmuz #173
Children of
HASHEM

Shmuz #174
The Illusion
of Reality

Shmuz #175
Rosh
Hashana Prep
- Yom Ha Din

Shmuz #176
Teshuvah
Shmuz 5769
- A Diamond
with a Flaw

Shmuz #177
Being Grate-
ful

Shmuz #178
To one person
you may
be the
whole world

Shmuz #179
The
Commit-
ments
of a Jew

Shmuz #180
Why We Want
Mosiach Now

Shmuz #181
Emunah
in Difficult
Times

Shmuz #182
Tolerating
Evil: A Per-
spective on Re-
cent Events

Shmuz #183
With Perfect
Faith: Bitachon
in Turbulent
times

Shmuz #184
The Galus
Mentality

Responsibility

Shmuz #185
Responsibility

Shmuz #186
G-d for the
Perplexed

Shmuz #187
Self Mastery-
The Key to
Good Middos

Shmuz #188
Rich Man
Poor Man -
The Ferris
Wheel of Life

Shmuz #189
Encounters
with G-d

Shmuz #190
My Rebbe

Shmuz #191
Combating
Robotic Juda-
ism

Shmuz #192
HASHEM
really cares

Shmuz #193
A Clash of
Civilizations

Shmuz #194
Tisha B'Av-
What we can
do to bring
the Geulah

Shmuz #195
Stop Playing
G-d!

Shmuz #196
I'd be the
first to Thank
HASHEM if

Shmuz #197
Teshuvah
Shmuz 5770
- Limiting
Beliefs

Shmuz #198
Life
Transforming
Moments

Shmuz #199
Lashon
Harah-
Mindless
Chatter

Shmuz #201
Chanukah
- The Power
given to Man

Shmuz #202
Outcomes
and
Intentions

Shmuz #203
Disney Land
USA, the ADD
Generation

Shmuz #204
Listening
to your
messages

Shmuz #205
The Giant
Within

Shmuz #206
Teshuva
Shmuz

Shmuz #209
Generation
W

Shmuz #211
Putting G-d
back into
Religion

Shmuz #213
The Tiny
Giant called I

Shmuz #214
Hashem
waits for our
Teshuva

Shmuz #216
Love the Life
You Live

Shmuz #217
The Incredible
Power of
Prayer

Theshmuz
on Bitachon